T0268377

HotWife
A Modern Fetish

A True Story

Mila Guerrerra

HotWife

© 2024 Mila Guerrerra

ISBN 979-8-35094-071-8

eBook ISBN 979-8-35094-072-5

Table of Contents

Introduction

My story is so hard to tell, and can be shocking to other people. It is something so private and delicate that I have gripped it to my heart. My story is between me and God, for very specific reasons. Everything that I have encountered in my life has been a build-up. The obstacles, the people, the problems, the deception that I have encountered felt like they were meant to derail my own path. To keep me in doubt, stuck and stagnant, from living. From becoming the person I was created to be. This story, and my ability to speak about my own life has freed me. I didn't choose to heal. The pain was driving everything in my life. And I needed peace. It connected me to the divine in me. Healed my soul.

Take only what connects to you.

It is important to note: this is my experience. There is absolutely nothing wrong with you – if you and your partner are safely, happily active in HotWifing, swinging or whatever it is that floats your boat. Every relationship, couple or marriage is beautiful and unique. Lifestylers and couples and 'experts' online will tell you that swingers and HotWife couples have emotionally healthy relationships. They tell you that it's great and exciting and normal. I cannot speak for other HotWives, I can only share what I know personally. My twenty year marriage did not make it. This is the part that nobody talks about. It took every ounce of courage and strength to share my journey, my wounds, my brokenness with you. I am still healing.

HotWifing is a modern fetish that for some reason is going more mainstream. It's a taboo where the husband gives his wife permission to have sex with other men. These men are known as "Bulls." This kink can be enticing to open minded couples that want to openly explore the world of kinky sex practices, specifically where the husband desires his wife to fuck another man. He gets off on the idea of her getting it on with other partners.

HotWifing was not the only catalyst to my divorce. My husband and I had the same marital issues that most couples have – home, finances, kids, parenting, dinner, pets, family, my family, his family. We were different, culturally. He is white, I am Latina. We had different values. Different beliefs. We could not communicate. We drifted away from each other. We had a laundry list of issues.

HotWifing is what broke me. It broke my heart. My body. My soul.

This is just a small piece of my story. I've survived so much, and somehow there is still more fight in me. I don't acknowledge this in my daily life the way I should. I don't honor it the way I should. But I am one million percent insanely proud of myself.

If you are in a relationship and taking the steps to openly and honestly communicate about the possibility of HotWifing, I hope this helps you. If you are recovering from being a HotWife, I hope this heals you.

Chapter One

I feel it's pretty safe to say that most happily married couples have fantasized about having sex with another partner at some time in their normal, healthy marriage. Couples make lists – for fun, "My Top Ten." Those sexy celebrities, rockstars, athletes, the sexy UPS drivers, trashy romance novels. These are sexy imaginings and private jokes with your love. All of this is part of a normal, healthy, intimate relationship. Most happily married women would not act on some of those fantasies. But some couples do. Imagining it and living it are two different things.

The HotWife is an alluring woman whose husband encourages and allows her to have sex with other men. He loves her so much, he wants others to know her and give her pleasure. She wears an anklet. A cute piece of jewelry that doubles as a signal that she is available to others in the lifestyle.

She is Me. An attractive Latina with olive skin, long curly brown hair and full lips, poised and well spoken. My features were different, unintentionally seductive and mysterious. This side always had my husband's focus. Qualities that always made me easily stand out. A light that shined from the inside out. A type of energy that can be magnetic to some people. Or the type of energy that certain people would be envious of or even try to diminish. A combination of sensitive and sassy. Very passionate about life, dedicated and loyal to family. I have always been introspective and attuned to my emotions with a high level of spiritual awareness. I could see the good in others, and it emanated outward. When people saw how I walked, how I moved, I unknowingly commanded their attention. I would look at other people and wonder, *Why are you staring at me?* But it had nothing to do with my external appearance. People are intrigued by what they cannot see – spirit, heart and empathy. They liked what I was made of, an energy that could not be bought or duplicated.

I grew up with a young, single mother and a dad that was in and out of our lives. I grew up with a strong sense of family, faith and pride. When my mother remarried, I moved across the country. We left the east coast and headed south. Inevitably, someone would ask, "Where are you from?" Really and truly, the question they were really asking is "Why do you look like that?"

I met my future husband when I was nineteen years old, in the early 1990's. He clearly had a thing for Latina's. We had a friendship and a long relationship before we were married. I was young but I had dated some. I had a serious boyfriend for a couple of years and a small group of good girlfriends. Rick was like no one I had met: a couple of years older and a really nice guy, with an edgy sense of humor. He always made me laugh and everyone liked him. I kept him in the friend zone for a bit. I was still feeling him out. We had a mutual group of work friends and had been out in a group setting many times. We would have dinners drinks, spend time with friends, ride go karts, attend baseball games, go rollerblading, attend concerts and festivals, all the fun stuff! We talked and laughed a lot. We had similar tastes in music and movies. He liked adventure. We were always on the go. We traveled – we partied – we smoked. Letting my guard down with him was easy in the beginning. We shared time. Moments. Dreams. Love. And we had a lot of sex. I had a better than good guy! I was over-the-moon happy. I was living and loving my twenties! I opened him to a completely different world. I shared the best parts of myself, my culture, and my family. I showed him a world of love, hope, faith and family. Different from his experience. We were inseparable and eventually moved in together.

Early in our relationship, when we were out with friends or at dinner, he noticed how other men would look at me or treat me. It turned him on. We would be at a gathering or driving home, and he would say "I saw that guy looking at your ass all night". He would insinuate that my girlfriend's husband would love to have sex with me. That didn't mean anything to me; I was with him. But I completely fed into it. We were young and feral. We were twenty something's. I thought, *My guy thinks I am so hot – that he notices that other people see me as hot!* He made me feel beautiful, desired, sexy and loved. We were young and exploring private bedroom talk, just he and I. It felt safe at the time.

Once we were invited to a work party at his manager's home. It was a casual spring weekend gathering. My outfit was simple, a classic white tee and cute skirt. We attended and enjoyed the day. We sat outside with other guests, enjoyed drinks and food overlooking the pool. Rick's boss formed an instant crush on me and chatted me up during the party. I caught him staring at me several times. He seemed to be putting himself wherever I was. I acted accordingly. I said things like, "You have a lovely home – 'dinner was great' – 'thanks for inviting us!"

The Monday following the party, my then – boyfriend came home to tell me I made an impression. Everyone wanted to know more about him and his beautiful girlfriend. I didn't understand the attention, I didn't perceive myself as beautiful, I took it as a compliment. The experience completely inflated and fueled his ego.

When Rick and I were alone together, I always wore lingerie, sexy nighties. I wanted to please him. He liked porn. I honestly didn't think anything of it. It was just normal. Something all guys did. He bought me different sex toys. He was sex driven. *Aren't most men?* He expressed love through sex.

We lived together for years and had talked about marriage. I even moved to another state to be with him and then moved back to our home state. In my eyes and in my heart we were solid.

I don't believe that he had any intention of HotWifing so early in our relationship, or that he even knew what it was. I don't think HotWife even became a word till the mid 2000's. My current adult self wonders if his actions were intentional. I did not see them as the Red Flags that I one day would.

Chapter Two

Rick and I whisked off to a tropical island to be married on a beautiful beach, just he and I, and it was wonderful. Our morning wedding ceremony was at the edge of the crystal blue water, and it was beautiful, romantic and everything I ever wanted. We had a special dinner on our wedding night. When we returned from our wedding trip, we had a festive family celebration. It was the next chapter in our lives. We were now Mr. and Mrs. All Grown Up! We exchanged parties and going out to start a family. I was making changes – no smoking or drinking. We cooked healthy dinners at home, I learned about yoga and began taking regular classes. I wanted to become a yoga teacher. We had a better-than-good sex life. When we were in our early thirties, we welcomed our first child, bought our first house. We had friends, extended family and were active in our community. Life was so good. Two years after our first child, we were overjoyed to be expecting again. This time we were having twins. We were building our lives together.

When you have a young family, your intimate relationship becomes disrupted with new demands. *What sex life?* If you have or had small children, you already know. You experience so many highs and so many lows. One minute you feel like you aren't going to make it. You wonder how you will make it through the day. Piles of laundry, baby puke, baby poop, diapers, late night feedings and sleepless nights. Then the next minute you are overwhelmed with feelings of pure joy, love and gratitude for your babies' precious smiles, first words, and cuddles. I loved every minute of it. It was my most favorite time of my life! Being the best mother I could be to my little cubs was top priority in my life, and it still is. Despite the sleep deprivation, work and everyday challenges I was so very happy. We were actively working on our relationship. Rick and I were still having sex, just once every seven to ten days.

Motherhood was my main priority. I had three littles – with constant needs. The house felt like a hurricane all the time; there was often not enough time to empty the dishwasher or pick up the kitchen in between the next set of bottles and bath time, let alone picking up the toys. Rick worked ten-hour days not including the commute. He was there in the morning before babies woke, and arrived home for bedtime cuddles and kisses. I was slowing down. My body changed, my outlook on life changed. I was working four days a week in an office. There were constant mom demands, eventually it made more sense to stay home. I had no idea how busy stay home moms were with preschool, school, teacher conferences, well checks, sick visits. We had financial ups and downs. His family visits every couple of months, always tense. We were coping with new levels of tiredness.

Right around the holidays, when our baby twins were seven months old, and the oldest was three, I found out I was pregnant again. It was one of the few times we did have sex during that period of time. I was late. Or was I? *Wait, when was the last time I got my period? What the hell?* We were busy parents of three littles, under the age of three. I had other things going on in my life and tracking my cycle wasn't one of them. I was on birth control. And I was breastfeeding. I peed on the stick. My knees buckled. My heart sank. Positive.

My mother called me the morning I peed on the stick. I was still in the bathroom. I answered, my quiet voice trembled, she immediately said, "What's wrong?" Without hesitation, "I responded I am pregnant and I am not keeping it." There was no way. I was seven months postpartum. I consulted with my doctor. I trusted and loved her. She delivered my children and took the best care of me. I had her support – and her recommendations so I made the arrangements.

A somber drive into the city. We drove around the block a couple of times. A group of protestors were camped in front of the building. *Fuck.* There was only one way into the clinic, and only one way out. We parked and walked together arm in arm. There was no getting past them. A conservative, older woman with long stringy hair slowly marched toward us. She wore a dark skirt, a sweater, her neck adorned in a large cross. There were two people walking behind her. I could feel my husband's energy shrink. I was not going to be intimidated. I needed to be protected. I needed him to see me, to see the situation. *Oh, Hell No,* I thought. I felt a fury and heat build inside me. I did not recognize the voice that came out of me. "YOU STAY THE FUCK BACK!" It felt like a growl and it got bigger. I picked up my pace and started to walk directly at her. I pointed my finger at her, again. YOU STAY THE FUCK OUT OF MY WAY YOU CRAZY BITCH. STAY THE FUCK BACK. I felt my husband's pace pick up so we could quickly walk pass.

I was shaking from the confrontation. My throat was raw. My blood pressure was off the charts. We checked in for a long day ahead. I don't remember much thereafter. I went home to rest. To heal. To be mommy to my three littles that were home waiting for me.

Healing from abortion is different for all women. The body has to heal. You have to find peace first, then make peace with yourself. It is a significant, life changing event in a woman's life. After a few weeks, it was easy for my husband to forget. Women – we don't forget. We remember, always.

I don't care where you stand on abortion. It was the right choice for me. Every woman deserves the right to choose whether or not if abortion is right for her. I will forever be thankful for the access I had to safe and legal abortion.

Chapter Three

Like most marriages, ours matured, we grew and evolved. Rick and I had not been this version of ourselves before. We were making new friends and growing as a couple as we were raising our family. We were doing the best we could. I would take time for myself by hitting the gym and taking yoga classes. He would escape through video games and golf. Rick needed constant stimulation from the outside world. We still celebrated life, birthdays and vacations together and were committed to our family. We were so intertwined. He often mistook my light for his light.

But our relationship was getting a little cold. I began to feel as though the only time I got attention or affection was for sex or during sex. I joked many times that our dog got more attention than I did (which was true). He would laugh at my joke. Rick was not good at reading between the lines. I felt that our marriage was still strong, that we were in the season of raising our littles. *It's just that time in our lives.* That's what I told myself anyway. My responsibility was my family. As kids do, mine grew quickly. They became more independent.

When my husband first brought up the HotWife fantasy, I didn't think anything of it. I loved him, and trusted him. In my thought process, there was no way we would actually go through it. I mean what man wants to share his wife? I understood a man wanting to show his woman off. Some men want to have other men be jealous of the woman he has. When a man walks into a room with a beautiful woman, everyone notices.

I personally had not heard of HotWifing when he broached the subject with me. Was it like swinging? Because that was a hard no for me. The topic made its way into our bedroom though dirty talk. Another way to spice up our bedroom life. We were communicating openly and taking the time to care for each other's needs. I had no intention of ever going through with it. But he began to drop hints.

Eventually, my curiosity got the better of me. I needed to know what this was, for myself. What exactly was this that he was talking about? *Real people can't actually do this, do they?* I did some research. I found some general information online. It was all about women – being sexually free, fulfilling their own fantasies. Couples celebrate the wife's beauty and increase their intimacy. Partners learning all about themselves – and each other. "Claim your sexual power," the website said. Looking back now I think, *What a load of crap that is! What man came up with all that?*

At the same time, the Christian Grey adult books were getting popular. It seemed relevant, if you would. Sexual fetishes were going mainstream. Then the movie came out and reached an even wider audience. This entire genre was so popular at the time. Frankly, HotWifing started to feel normal because it mirrored somewhat the things I was seeing in the media. I would go out with girlfriends and someone would ask, "Are you reading the books?" I personally had not read them, but I knew all about them. My monthly girls night out was always so fun! I loved going out and looked forward to these get-togethers as a mini escape from my mom duties. I missed getting dressed up – and enjoyed the laughs. It felt fun to have my little HotWife secret for my husband and I – it was just ours. In my mind, there was no way he would actually want this. I was his, and he was mine. *Real people don't do that!* But he didn't stop dropping the hints.

My husband also liked porn. A lot. He had some magazines, and VHS tapes. Hell, I watched with him. Pre-kids, pre-marriage, I didn't think much of it. I would walk in on him, and catch him on the computer. He would quickly shut it down – When I would say "Aha, I saw that!" He would laugh, shut it down. It was no big deal, it was just something that guys did. Rick had shared that when he was young, his father hid his porn magazines in his toolbox in the garage. As we were growing together, and life and technology evolved, I believe porn is where he discovered his HotWife fantasy.

No matter where you stand on pornography, the point is: it is not real. Porn is not reality. Porn is not real sex. It creates a false expectation. It is harmful to one's well being, mental health and soul health. My husband did not understand the difference between sex and intimacy. I feel his porn addiction shaped our reality. It went beyond the bedroom and perpetuated his desire to find fulfillment outside the relationship rather than being in the relationship and working on it. Porn is a thief of intimacy. There are multiple studies, statistics, articles, detailing harmful effects of porn to people, relationships and society. Do your own research on the long term effects of pornography and decide for yourself.

During this period of our lives, I thought he was happy in our relationship. I was wrong. The first time he slipped, he hurt me terribly. He left an email open on our computer. A message to one of my long distance girlfriends, Sarah. He didn't know her – he knew of her. She had kids the same age as ours, and was going through a divorce. I was one of her few friends, and I loved her dearly. He knew she and I chatted frequently and that we were close. He was present sometimes when she and I would have late night chats with wine after we put our kids to bed. Somehow, Rick hijacked my friendship, right under my nose. He forgot to shut his computer down. They had an email chain; the messages flirty and full of innuendo. I was stunned. *What in the actual fuck was happening?! Why did he have her email? What the hell else did he talk to her about?!* I immediately confronted him. I was beyond angry. *How dare he!* "What the fuck do you think you are doing?" We argued in the garage that night, so we wouldn't wake our kids. I was upset; I was pissed; I was hurt. I was shocked that he betrayed me like that. The breath knocked out of me. I stayed in bed for a couple of days recovering from the sadness. I lied to my kids, Mommy is sick. I hate lying.

He swore! Rick swore up and down that it would never happen again. It crushed me. I honestly don't know how he managed to gaslight me and manipulate the situation. I didn't know those words back then. But he knew what he was doing. He knew messaging my friend like that was wrong and he still did it anyway. We managed to work through it. I tucked it away. I ended the friendship with my girlfriend but – I forgave Rick. Our sex life survived. Our relationship went on. But it was not the same. I was not the same. My trust was broken. The foundation of our relationship was cracked. It was a bitterly painful experience.

I didn't want to lose him, so I started to lose myself. It was the beginning of a standard that I set: I was willing to maintain this marriage at my own expense. I wanted to believe that my marriage was strong, that it could survive anything. I kept my pain private. I avoided my family. I picked up my broken pieces and went on. I did not share this secret with anyone for many years. I didn't want anyone to know. I was embarrassed and afraid of what those closest to me would say. That shame was too much.

Forgiveness is a huge challenge. I couldn't just snap my fingers and erase the hurt. I didn't care about myself enough to really deal with it. I felt like I was in my marriage alone. I did not know how out of alignment I was with myself. To me, marriage was forever. Anything worth doing takes care, communication, commitment, compromise and focus. With that comes the work, routines, difficulties and disappointments. For better or worse, good times and bad, sickness and health. We pushed through.

There were so many good times in between the bad times. I began running on autopilot. Our routine was normal. Everything I was used to before Rick's infidelity remained the same. The bedroom HotWife chatter, the porn. In fact, Rick sank deeper into the HotWife obsession. His porn addiction was a real one. I had no idea what type of deep dives he would make when he was online. He would share a little, here and there. I naively trusted him. I was still feeling the effects of the email betrayal with my friend. I was overwhelmed with feelings of what I could do to make sure my husband didn't do this again. He was always pushing the edge. He was leading us into territory that we knew nothing about.

Chapter Four

I didn't know anything about the HotWife lifestyle. Rick, on the other hand, had learned quite a bit. He had an account on a milder porn website and created an account for me too, and linked them together. We were "friends" on the account. My account name was 'Latina HotWife' and the profile picture was of my anonymous legs in these gorgeous black and white designer stockings. Yes, I allowed him to take pictures. They were for him. He promised my face would never be in any of the pictures. Since it was just my legs, I was okay with using that as our shared profile picture. I loved the stockings, and the way my legs looked in them. It was an ego boost for me. It felt good for him to validate that I was still beautiful, sexy and he was proud of his wife. For me, at the time it was fun and harmless. I wanted so badly to be connected to my husband. Through our accounts, he would forward me pictures of the fantasy that was ruling our bedroom. I totally participated. It was a new way of connecting. It became how we communicated.

One day, he told me he made contact through the website. A friend. His new friend's name was 'J-Bird,' an unhappily married professional male. He lived in our state, just a few hours away. He had an old girlfriend in our area. *A wife and a girlfriend?* A wife that didn't know he had a girlfriend. I didn't know what to think. He and Rick became acquainted, exchanged conversation, lifestyle stories, photos of us. He was normal looking in his photos. Normal everyday pics of himself, his girlfriend, his dick. I admit, he was nice looking in his pictures. He seemed similar to us, and he was actually living this lifestyle. *Interesting.*

My husband invited me to talk to him. *Ok, wow!* I thought. I was surprised because I never planned to actually engage in real life. *But okay, why not?* He lived four hours away, and we weren't actually going to meet. We began a group chat, the three of us. Eventually, J-Bird and I took our conversation to private messaging – husband arranged and approved. We became online friends. Online friends who would exchange selfies and conversation everyday. The conversation was sweet and nice. He complimented me. Made me feel pretty. Harmless, right? I began to look forward to my daily flirtation with him. I was getting attention that I was not getting in my daily life. I was getting more attention from my email boyfriend than I was getting from my husband. Our conversations were good. I started to like them too much.

Email exchanges with J-Bird became more intense. It became sexting. He made me feel sexy and good. I was not prepared to handle the impact. I was addicted to this conversation. It began to feel like I was betraying my husband. I knew in the back of my mind – inappropriate conversation with someone, who was not my husband could be considered cheating in a committed relationship.

Cheating comes in many forms: online affairs, physical affairs, emotional ones, sexual ones. It took a couple of years for me to have that realization and understand how I personally defined cheating. Everyone has their own definition.

During the year or so I was chatting with J-Bird, it never occurred to me to ask what or who my husband was doing online. My work/life balance was slim. I had my kids, husband and work to attend to, and I would do it all over again the next day. I began to lose touch with reality. My husband made all this feel so normal. When you hear the same phrases over and over again, it becomes your reality. I was so lonely in my marriage. I felt ashamed of what was happening in my relationship. I had no one to talk to about it. When I went out with girlfriends, I remained silent about the online relationship my husband had set up for me. Would any of my happily married girlfriends relate to any of this? I could never tell anyone. The stigma that could come with sharing what I was going through could be damaging to my reputation in my community. I pulled further and further away from my family and friends.

I began to feel embarrassed and unworthy. I would ask Rick, "Am I not pretty enough for you? Am I gaining weight?" Intrusive thoughts swirled in my brain – and began to take over. A sadness began to form. I became more insecure in my marriage. I felt invisible to my husband. I only received attention if it was related to sex. I had to ask for hugs. Affection is normal, healthy and essential in romantic relationships.

I would attempt to have a conversation with Rick, I wanted to know the reason for his desires and actions. What was the motivation behind them "Why are we doing this?" I would ask. "Do you love me? Are you happy? Why do you want to give me away?" To which he would respond, "This is a no drama situation. We can stop any time." *Was that his way of being supportive?*

Rick could never answer my question. I felt like I was being silenced. He gave me little to no eye contact during these conversations. The lack of concentration and attention made me feel painfully small and ignored. He made me feel needy for wanting his attention. He had a roundabout way of talking that was frustrating and would withdraw from the conversation as quickly as he could. He was impatient and lacked empathy. Not listening was his way of ignoring the difficult things I wanted to talk about.

Guilt, shame and confusion were beginning to run a course through my entire being. My husband was incapable of having conversations like this, anything that required going deeper than surface level. I felt like I was insulting him by bringing up my concerns because another part of me thought he would never do anything to harm our marriage. He felt entitled to his desires – and would shut down any attempt at real communication. We would be upset, short with one another for a couple of days and then pick back up like nothing happened. He made me feel like I was the one creating drama. His energy was confusing. "I was just joking" was a common response if he hurt my feelings or "You take everything the wrong way." Every time I would speak up, I was disturbing his peace. He wasn't available. He would not validate me. It felt like he thought I didn't have a right to be angry. He didn't understand, could not put himself in my shoes. The conversation would then get twisted, or he would say something passive aggressive and shut me down. Arguing was easier for him. What I needed was for him to pick me up, hold me, hug me. To say, "I love you babe."

Why was that so hard?

I was communicating the only way I knew how to at the time. I was a good woman, a good mother and a good wife. To him, I was nagging, complaining and being difficult because I was expressing myself. I was always there for him. I always came through for him.

I knew he worked hard at a stressful job with long hours. I was only asking for simple respect and communication. He made me feel like I was high maintenance. But really and truly he was incapable of showing up for me, for my needs. It's okay to have healthy expectations of your partner. Kindness, love and compassion. After he repeatedly dismissed my feelings, I slipped deeper inward. I just wanted my husband and my life back. I felt cutoff.

My online relationship with J-Bird ran its course. He didn't truly know me. It was just an outlet to make myself feel better. I had to let it go. I knew we weren't going to meet in person, and it simply wasn't worth it. Even though I was married to Rick. It felt like a breakup. I missed his "Good morning Gorgeous" messages.

Discussion, healthy conflict, conversation and compromise are part of all relationships. My husband thought these conversations were drama and would divert. No Drama, really and truly, he did not want it to stop. I tried to step right back into what I thought was my normal life. It worked for a little while. I felt my life changing. Everything felt like an argument. Whether it was our kids, house, money, paint, dinner, my family, his family. We still loved one another but it was changing. Something was beginning to ache deep in me. We still made it work partly because I refused to open my eyes. I refused to see myself. I was abandoning myself for the sake of Rick's attention, for his approval. I was completely disconnected from the part of me that needed purpose and meaning in my life. Every part of you deserves love, kindness, tenderness, grace. Even the parts of you that you may be ashamed of.

When my kids were elementary age, I found out I was pregnant. Again. I was shocked. I was in my late thirties. I was on the pill and I was diligent every day taking it in the morning. How was this happening to me. We had no intention of having another baby. I was past the diapers and potty training, I was beginning to feel human again. I didn't want to go back into maternity clothes, or late night feedings. But that little part of me inside, entertained the thought, for just a moment. *Could a baby bring us closer again? Or would a baby drive us further apart?*

I did not want to go through the abortion experience again. The thought of it made me shudder. Together we made the decision to end the pregnancy. We told no one. The day of the procedure, we kissed our kids and sent them to school. I was home by the time they got off school. Mommy was resting, she didn't feel well. Rick took the kids to the park and for ice cream. I laid in bed. I cramped. I hurt. I cried. I sobbed. I bled. I was alone. Twice. I was completely alone. Rick finally agreed to a vasectomy.

My body healed. I did my best to heal my heart. Women do not forget.

Chapter Five

My husband would not relinquish his HotWife fantasy. Even after I ended my online relationship, Rick's fantasy creeped back into our lives. I was lonely. I was sad. Rick encouraged me to pick up online conversations again. And I did. I was bored. Really, I was depressed. My husband only wanted me when other men were interested. I could not face that.

I felt like I had experience now. I wasn't blindly scrolling anymore, placating my husband. I had enough knowledge and strength that I could better explore my options this time. I had some online conversations. Men who were married, some exploring, some just messing around online.

An online connection turned into a real life lunch date, and a make out session in the parking lot of a restaurant. But it didn't feel good. It felt awkward and unnatural. I wanted to please my husband. I wanted him to want me. I wanted someone to love me – because I didn't love myself.

A drink with a tall creepy stranger who wanted to clamp my nipples. That scared the hell out of me. Back to square one. I stopped pursuing online relationships for a while. It was too much. I had a swift kick back into reality and remembered, *This could be dangerous.*

I still loved my life or rather the idea I had of how happy my life could be. I still loved my husband. I wanted him to show me he loved me too. Like he used to. As I watched my kids grow, and wanted so much for them – I wanted more in my life. I was seeking more. I didn't know what I was looking for – but whatever it was, I wasn't finding it. Not in my marriage, my circle of friends, my work – definitely not in the wine I was drinking or the weed I was smoking. I was changing into someone I didn't recognize. I was empty. We went on like this for years.

I was starving for a real connection. I was exclusive to him in my heart, and he could not give me the same commitment. I craved consistency and stability. I could no longer recognize my own feelings. I could not identify my own voice, my own integrity, my own self. The emotional deprivation brought with it lower self esteem, headaches, fatigue, overeating, overindulging and bad choices. I remember having a drinking lunch with girlfriends. We sat on a lovely patio, watching our kids play together downing margarita's. What was I thinking? I behaved in ways that do not align with my moral code.

My husband did not want to stop – and was not going to. Not until he got his fantasy fulfilled. He met David online. A happily married, professional average looking, early forties man. He was seeking a woman for a discreet friendship. My husband arranged it all. He wanted this. We had come this far. Ten years, if not more. I thought, if I gave Rick his fantasy he would finally be satisfied. I had to go through with it. I couldn't say no.

The three of us met for a drink: Rick, David and me. We met at a restaurant, halfway between our cities. Rick and I walked into the restaurant hand in hand. I immediately recognized him. I was thankful he looked better in person. David shook hands with my husband first, then he took my hand and pressed his cheek against my cheek, almost like a kiss, but not. *Was that charming or was it ballsy?* We ordered drinks. I don't remember having a drink before we left the house, but I know myself well enough to know that I must have slammed a glass of wine or two before we headed out. The three of us shared introductions and small talk.

David was nice. More importantly, he said all the right things. He loved his wife, his children and was not looking to change his situation. He just went outside of his marriage from time to time. This was clearly not his first time stepping outside of his marriage. He acknowledged that we are all human with families and loved ones. He understood the risk of people getting hurt, and would be respectful. David needed boundaries and discretion. He left cash for our drinks and left.

When I first began researching HotWifing, I learned that a big part of the build up for the woman is the anticipation for the date with her bull – getting ready for it. All I remember thinking was, Oh my God, over and over. I thought, *If I don't go through with the fantasy, I'll kill my marriage. If I do go through with it, I still kill it.*

I met David the next week for a drink and a kiss in the car. By the next week – I fucked him on the stairs at one of his properties. I came home to my husband to tell him I was finally his HotWife. The high from that experience lasted for a long time. It brought electricity back in our relationship.

That was the only experience with David, but it sustained my husband for a while. The fantasy of having sex with a stranger in a fancy house, bent over the stairs. My husband loved hearing every detail. I was so absent from my body that I felt like a robot. I was doing what my husband wanted. I was completely detached, disassociated. Not feeling anything. Completely physical.

But now, I could say we were wild and crazy. Now Rick and I had a great story for the nursing home. The HotWife experience only created a renewed, elevated sexual intensity for my husband. Going back to normal sex did not satisfy him. Our bond had changed. It wasn't broken, but it was different. I hoped that one tryst with David would satisfy my husband, but that backfired.

Some time had passed, but it began again. Rick dropped more hints. He continued to mention HotWifing in bed together. "It was time to start looking for another friend," he said. Following Rick's lead, I became further entangled in a downward cycle. I could not see how I was betraying myself.

Chapter Six

Thomas was a professional forty-something man from Iowa. He was unhappily married to a disabled woman. A conservative veteran, Ex-college football player. A dad. Involved in his church. To this day he is the only person I have ever met, in my entire life, that did not use swear words. We met a couple of times. The first time just to say hello. The second time, a scheduled encounter. A lonely man, Thomas, enjoyed wining and dining me. Occasionally, clarity would seize me and I would think, *What in the fucking hell am I doing?* But another part of me knew I was escaping from my husband. And I was doing what he wanted me to do. *I should try to enjoy myself.* I was dressed up – I looked great – but inside I was far from it. Really, I was sad and lonely. I was at an upscale restaurant – in an upscale hotel, because my husband would rather me be here, with this guy than at home with him. It wasn't about the sex anymore; the sex with Thomas was quick. I numbed. I drank more. I smoked more.

The next time Thomas was in town, I made up a story. "Mom is off to visit with an old friend in town just for tonight," I'd tell my kids Ugh! I was on the freakin' PTA! Right after work I would drink a mini bottle of wine on the way to rendezvous with Thomas for just a couple of hours. Worse, I found myself driving under the influence to get myself home. Thomas was more concerned about my drive home with a couple of glasses of wine in me – than my husband was, but letting the drink wear off was not an option. I had to head out. Home to have sex with my husband.

When I left Thomas, it was late. I had a thirty mile drive ahead of me. When he expressed concern, I said "I'm fine, good to go." I was sober enough, but walking a thin line. I drove with the windows down in the cold, music blasting. I brushed away intrusive thoughts of blue flashing lights appearing in my rearview mirror, visions of blowing into a breathalyzer. My mind raced with the risks I was taking. I prayed for angels to be with me.

Upon arriving home, I immediately poured an "I made it home" glass of wine. I felt tense and twisted from the anxious drive home, exhausted from my day at work, the sex I just had with Thomas. I had not seen my kids since early that morning when we started our day, I had not seen my husband. I was drunk and unshowered. Dirty. But it was time to fuck my husband.

The HotWife 'after sex' experience is when the husband takes his wife back. That's what I read about when I began learning on my own – what this kink was supposed to be. That was what drove my husband's lust. That's what he got off on. It was primal for him. He got off the most on fucking me while I was still full from my last tryst.

I was depleted. I had nothing left to give. I felt unclean, unsanitary. I was empty. Thank God I was numb from the wine and the weed. I didn't understand his desire for it. I don't want to understand his desire for it. It would take me a couple of days to recover. Not from the sex. From being robbed from my own precious energy. Weary from the mental gymnastics I was doing in my head. The thoughts would get even more invasive, more negative. I began to wonder if Rick was gay. I began to wonder if he was bisexual. I started to wonder if, during the times he traveled on business, if he was hooking up with random people. The pictures he took of me. The ones I trusted him to delete, was he showing them to other people? I couldn't go there. I managed to control my suspicious thoughts and hide them in some shadowy place. I talked myself out of seeing everything he was showing me.

It's cliché but true, I avoided looking at myself in the mirror. Rick oscillated between neglecting me and using me for sex. Instead of nourishing me with love and care, he brought the words "slut" and "whore" into the bedroom. I was not getting anything out of our sex, out of our relationship. My heart was breaking. I didn't want to lose him. I didn't know what I was feeling. I didn't want to feel whatever that I was. I became an unappreciated woman who kept getting mistreated. I got used to it. I regularly told myself, *It's fine, this is fine.* I would pick up my sad, broken self, put myself back together and go on like nothing happened.

Even though I felt weak and tired from the emotional roller coaster I was living, I would pour myself into my kids, my yoga practice, working out, hanging out with friends. I was beginning to evolve, not for better. I didn't like myself anymore. The thoughts in my head weren't going away. If I brought up concerns, Rick would downplay the tension. Downplay – the reality of the risks. "This is what works for us." Rick would mention friends or acquaintances, "I'll bet they are like us." He would divert to cope with my unhappiness by joking around. Part of me didn't want to believe that he could blatantly hurt me either, so I continued to cater to his desire.

It was just easier that way. To appease. He simply couldn't hear me and – he had conditioned me to do what he wanted me to do. I was beginning to accept this as normal. He paid the bills. He provided. We would talk about our relationship – and be flooded with happy memories of our younger selves, how happy and excited we were in the beginning. How in love we were. I would catch a glimpse of who he once was to me. How he presented himself pre-kids, pre-current reality. The contrast was overwhelming. Now I can see the truth – I was just playing a part that he created for me in his world.

Sadness and anxiety weighed me down. It was difficult to understand my own feelings. The heaviness in my heart was so intense. I showed so much love to everyone, a lot of compassion and empathy, but struggled to give myself the same. I was so tired. Most could not see the hardship I was going through. Ironically, some may have even thought that I had an easy, happy life, not knowing the emotional burdens that lived inside it.

Our relationship was getting tense. We were outgrowing our home. We became easily annoyed and impatient with another. I felt like my husband was becoming more distant, more defensive. He wasn't there for me emotionally. I felt invisible, unseen, unheard. I descended further inward. There was so much triggering energy all around me. I could sense that he was becoming uncomfortable around my presence. I was changing and highlighting the ugly parts within himself that he wasn't ready access

Chapter Seven

When Rick's parents would visit, they invoked tension for all of us. Rick and I would inevitably argue or fight. His family dynamic was so strange to me. He and his brother would always fight. When we were younger, they fought over stupid things. Brotherly competition. But it got ugly sometimes. It was as if they enjoyed antagonizing and one upping one another. Something that they never wanted to evolve past.

Sometimes, the way Rick presented himself to his family – was different from the way he showed up with me. He was an imposter in a mask. No one knew the side of Rick I did; he operated differently depending on who he was around.

He didn't have a positive support system around him, his family negatively affected him. They created a barrier in our connection. There was an undertone of disrespect with his family. He tried to come across unphased, confident, but I think it wore him down.

Rick used a lot of humor and sarcasm to avoid deeper feelings. He was a little shy about showing affection around his family. He tried to present himself as someone who was steady and unrattled.

I think he liked to be perceived as unfeeling. He could at will turn his feelings on and off. Did that make him feel more like a man? To present an exterior that was cold?

My relationship with Edna, my mother in-law, was uncomfortable. She was the type of woman that filled every room or car ride with constant chatter. She would babble about decorating, cooking, the politics of her church, gossip about people I didn't know or cared about. It was frustrating and annoying because she was often negative and rude about mostly everything. It was hard to maintain a back and forth conversation with her, even on shopping trips. We had nothing in common. I don't think she could relate to me. I always felt scrutinized by her.

Edna only had sons. I imagine it must have been lonely being the only woman in the house. She had stories of her son's crazy antics riding bikes, running around terrorizing the neighborhood as kids, getting in trouble because boys will be boys.

She ignored boundaries, just made herself right at home. Quick to tell you dinner was good, it just needed a little bit more of this or that. The dinner I shopped for, prepared, cooked. She would walk into the kitchen after I cleaned up with a smirk, "Oh, I guess I didn't time that right," Implying that she missed the opportunity to help me. Her microaggressions got so annoying that I dished back. I was starting not to care.

Edna definitely did not like brown or Black people. Once, as I sat at her kitchen table for an afternoon visit while my toddler was napping, she shared something about her Black neighbor, and punctuated it with – "You know, people of that breed." She chattered on and on, but I felt thrown by what she said. I had never heard anyone say such ugly words in real life. I brushed them off, what else could I do with my husband's mother? I shared my experience at her kitchen table with Rick later. No real reaction.

Another time, she sat in my house, on my couch, the evening news loud in the background, and she commented, "Oh, well it looks really dark over there." to a story playing on the news. I thought to myself, *Did she just make another racist comment?* I shot her a glare and she got up and left the room. I was doing my best to be a good wife. Thank God they lived out of state. Visits every couple of months would bring a dark cloud.

I am a Puerto Rican woman. My ethnicity is Hispanic. I have olive skin. I am bilingual. I come from a multi-ethnic mix of Spanish, African and Taino. My family is a beautiful rainbow of people, all different colors. Most of them were at my wedding reception. Who talks like that still? I told my husband how much her words upset me. "They're from another generation," he would say, "I'll talk to them about it."

The last racist comment my mother-in-law made in my presence surfaced in the car. She shared a recent uncomfortable experience at the dentist. She was very upset because the dental assistant had her 'big black boobs' too close to her during her cleaning. I looked at her and my face must have morphed. She said, "I know" as if my face signaled agreement with her racist reaction. I felt sickened and appalled by her comment. That type of behavior is intolerable to me.

My father-in-law was one of a kind. Not in a good way. I tried so hard to ignore this man, who was patriarchal, misogynistic, crude and entitled. He loved to share his opinions and didn't care if he insulted or upset people, kids included. If anyone shared a story of their experience, he pointed out what they should have said or should have done in that situation. When his glass emptied during family dinners, he would shake it toward his wife, a signal for her to refill it. His jokes always came at someone's expense. Gatherings with the entire family made humiliation and abusive jokes a sport. He was the type of person to enjoy making people feel dumb for being excited about something. I didn't want my kids to think this type of behavior was okay or to accept this type of behavior in their own future relationships. My eyes could not see that I was setting the worst example possible.

There were a few times in our marriage when we needed help. Like most young couples, you eat your pride and ask. My in-laws were able to provide the financial help we needed. In those moments, they were kind and generous, and I was thankful. They helped us when we needed it the most. But their generosity came with a price, a hidden contract. It felt like we became enslaved to them. I had to bite my tongue and smile.

Our immediate family began to dread their visits. Even Rick would get tense. Each time they came, I found myself getting sick. It was as if my entire body was rejecting them before they even arrived. I would get headaches, or belly aches. We would all breathe a sigh of relief when they headed home.

Chapter Eight

Two to three years, maybe more, had passed since I had thought of my old email boyfriend, "J-Bird." To my surprise, he reached out. His real name was James. He found himself working in my part of the state and was only thirty minutes away. Everything rushed back to me. He was my first stop on my HotWife journey, back when it felt new and playful. His emails always made me feel good. I had been feeling so low and now I was enjoying this much needed ego boost. James had always been good at lifting my spirits. I shared with my husband that he reached out. He was surprised, but of course he was okay with it.

James and I met at a local bar in my neighborhood. I had been there several times for dinner, drinks and live music with my husband and circle of friends. It was a weeknight, and chances that anyone I knew would see me with him were slim. But there was still a possibility. A stupid choice, but I was already making stupid decisions.

I instantly recognized him. James was attractive, like I remembered, and tall. He walked with an overbearing sense of self confidence. We walked toward one another in the parking lot, greeted each other with a hug. We had good conversation and good drinks. He liked booze more than me, which was saying something. I quickly realized he was an alcoholic. I wasn't judging. I just felt surprised. It didn't translate over email. He still had a wife and family four hours away. He worked and lived between two cities. We ended the evening with some parking lot kissing and a plan to get together again in near future. I went home to my husband.

A few weeks later, Thomas messaged me. He would be back in my city and wanted to meet. With my husband's approval, we planned our regular rendezvous. As always, I texted Rick – the hotel room number and I returned home to cater to him.

The next evening, James sent an email. It was a long weekend, and I was enjoying the night resting having dinner with Rick and the kids, the TV on in the background. I was playing on my phone when his notification appeared on my screen. It was an invitation, "Come to my bed tonight." He made me feel gorgeous and sexy in his messages. I showed my husband. With lust in his eyes Rick said, "Can you fuck three men in one weekend?" *What in the actual hell was I doing?* I thought. I had my visit with Thomas the night before, and had already been with my husband. What did it say about me if I was with three men in one weekend?

James agreed to meet me halfway. When I hopped in his car, he seemed a little off, but I didn't really know him. He had been drinking, but so had I. He was renting an apartment attached to a barn in an exclusive equestrian community, he said. We took a thirty-minute drive back to his place – dark and winding country roads. Each turn, combined with the wine I already consumed, made me feel tense. I didn't know where I was going. There were no other cars on the road. Fear began to rush over me. *He could kill me and leave me in the woods.* I snapped into hypervigilance. The realness of what I was doing. He could have been an insane serial killer. My mind became acutely aware of everything. But we arrived at his apartment, exactly where he said it would be. The first thing I noticed as we walked in was a giant jug of vodka on the counter. James wasted no time. I felt how much bigger he was than me as he kissed and undressed me. It felt sloppy. Trashy. Cheap. Not like I wanted it too. It didn't feel sexy like his emails. He didn't feel like the man that I had exchanged selfies, stories and sexting. I was so disappointed in myself. James took me back to the car. That was the last I would ever see him.

When I got home, I catered to my husband. It was the last time I would be a HotWife.

Chapter Nine

The energy shifted. Something was different in me. Something was different in Rick. I felt an exhaustion deep in my bones even deeper in my heart. I didn't want to have sex with my husband. I didn't feel loved by him, so how could it possibly feel good or natural?

It took about a week after my last HotWife experience with Rick, Thomas and James – for my body to start breaking down. My self-worth and my emotional wellbeing were completely gone. My immunity was low. I was dehydrated. I was depleted and broken. I became agitated and tense. I was the worst version of myself that I had ever been. I felt as if somehow I made this happen, it was my own fault.

I was resisting the truth so hard. And so was my body. Something felt wrong. I was beginning to unravel. I was no longer able to keep my suspicious thoughts tucked away. I felt like my husband was changing the rules. He was making them up as he went along for his convenience. I couldn't read my own intuition over his hot and cold behavior. Rick showed little interest in daily life and less interest in anything I had to say. Those intrusive thoughts were no longer intrusive. What used to sound like a whisper, began to scream in my ear. The thoughts came with a quick, sharp bolt of pain, triggering a headache with a deep pain behind my eye.

One day Rick casually mentioned, as I feared, that he had been chatting with someone. "My friend Kayla from college found me online." There was no doubt in my mind he was up to nothing good. I started to lose sleep. A slow fire began to brew deep inside me. I was more on edge because his parents would arrive for a visit soon.

Rick's disregard and lack of care was weighing heavier. Headaches came more frequently. I was withdrawing more. I was troubled. I was fighting the lies I was living by. These new reactions confirmed that everything that I felt was real and valid. I couldn't help but question Rick's motives and the patterns I had been willfully ignoring over the years to make our marriage work.

Rick mentioned a female co-worker, Anni, in another state. *Why does he know that she's getting a boob job?* Later he shared that she was cheating on her husband. They took their conversation outside of work hours. *Why is he only making connections with women?* The only other male person in his life was his brother, there were no other guys he called friends. I always trusted Rick up until this point. He was so friendly to everyone. For the first time, my perception changed. Now, his friendliness seemed calculated. Predatorial. Our circle of friends was my group of friends. He mostly played golf with his brother, video games with online people or the occasional hunting trip. His one childhood friend lived in another state.

How long had he been talking with these women? What were they talking about? Was he talking about me, about us?

One night, I went to bed early, to rest my body. I was worn out. The headache and pain accelerated quickly. The feelings I had buried away deeply just so I could get through the days were marching in my mind. I was processing so much, suddenly able to see all his actions clearly for the first time. Was he like this entire marriage? Or was I seeing him differently? *What the hell was going on?*

The morning my in-laws were arriving, I dropped the kids off at school and headed to work. I was feeling sick and out of sorts. But I pushed myself forward. I pushed through what I was feeling in my body. I should have stayed home.

Why do we do this to ourselves as women?

Something wasn't right with me. I called Rick from work. He didn't answer. *He's just with his parents*, I thought. I couldn't focus. Flashes of light, warning signs of a new migraine shot in my head, made me dizzy and disoriented. My right eye went blurry. I was in an immense amount of pain and was in the office alone. *Was I having a heart attack?* I couldn't catch my breath. Stabbing pains shot in the back of my head. Bolts of light would strike and make me wince and whine. I managed to call an eye doctor while gripping my eye and supporting my head on my desk. I got an appointment. But not until late in the day. I still couldn't reach Rick. I didn't think I could drive myself home. I couldn't sit – I couldn't stand – I couldn't think. I had to leave work. I couldn't tolerate the pain or the sunlight shining through the clouds. I should not have driven. It felt like my eyeball was trying to jump out of my head. I prayed. I prayed hard. I prayed to drive safely as I gripped the wheel with one hand – held my hand over my eye with the other. I don't know how I made it home. Likely the same angels that guided me home those HotWife nights.

I came home to an empty house. I collapsed into my bed, crying in agony. I couldn't move. My head down to my toes, everything in my body was screaming. I rolled into a little ball and pulled the covers over my head.

Rick came home and woke me. He spent the day with his parents. It was time to go to the ophthalmologist. The last appointment of the day. Upon my examination, I covered my good eye, so I could tell him how many fingers he was holding. I could see nothing. Not even a shadow. I could barely focus on the doctor's words. The pressure in my eye socket elevated beyond any normal level. He scheduled surgery at 6:00AM the next morning to add a drainage tube behind my retina. My medical diagnosis was traumatic iritis. Symptoms come on suddenly and bring chronic inflammation, pain, light sensitivity, headaches and decreased vision.

I was in and out of sleep and pain. I was alone in my own darkness. The surgery, scheduled first thing the next day, left me with an eye patch, bruising and swelling, day eye drops, night eye drops, eye gel, pain medication and zero vision in my right eye. I was a sad mess. For the first time, I was knocked down so hard, I could not move. I was at my worst. I saw the kids in between naps. They didn't know what to do. I love you and feel better mom. Rick drove me to the doctor's appointments. The doctor monitored the dangerously high pressure in my eye, there was a possibility of losing my eye. *What?* I couldn't grasp the seriousness of my condition at the time.

I spent the next week in and out of sleep in a state of pain, darkness,isolation and sadness I had never experienced. I could not tolerate any light. I couldn't get out of bed. It brought a heightened awareness in my body, my senses, my emotions. I was unable to use my phone even on the lowest brightness setting. I was in a dark stupor. Rick was at work most of the day, but when he was home, he made sure I had my medicine, water and snacks at my bedside table. I wished he would just lay with me. Hold me. Hug me. Tell me everything is going to be okay.

He did not.

Once I was settled, he would leave me alone in our lonely bedroom. I felt as though I was an inconveneince. I was so accustomed to the way he treated me, but there was a hope in me that he would find it in his heart to see how much I needed him. *Did he forget that he loved me?* But I couldn't think about that. I needed rest. I slept, quietly cried or I prayed.

I believe my illness was my body's way, God's way of getting my attention and saying "Open your eyes." The pain was so loud it had all my attention. My universe was falling apart. Everything was completely outside of my control, like God intervened to preserve my own sacredness. It invited me to replay the hardest moments in my marriage. I was being forced to surrender. It didn't look like it and it certainly didn't feel like it, but I believe I was being protected from a tragic outcome. This was the big and powerful catalyst that woke me up.

I found myself wondering, *How did I get here? How did this happen?* I was in a cocoon experiencing a frightening metamorphosis. The process my body underwent would be the most powerful and potent of my life. I watched a replay of how I arrived at that moment. I was remembering, reminiscing, realizing. I journeyed deep inside and looked at everything I didn't want to see. I felt everything that I did not want to feel. I felt it all so hard in my entire body and being. Everything I was running from, my own intuition, my fear, my doubt, my insecurities – I just sat with them. I was too weak to fight it. I could do nothing but just be with the murkiness behind my eyes. I had no choice but to feel it all. It wrecked my body and being. Something was dying in me. Behind my closed eyes, I deconstructed and reconstructed my life experiences.

Forgotten memories, forgotten for a reason. Unpleasant pranks, little tricks he played. Things only he thought were funny. Off putting. Why did I forget? I remembered a time before we were married. We were enjoying a summer day, boating with friends. He jumped off the boat, and pretended not to come back up. After several minutes of calling his name, one of the men became concerned, Rick popped up out of the water. Why would he even consider that funny?

I would cry myself to sleep, wake a few hours later, and take a regiment of prescriptions from steroids, pain medication, eye drops, eye gel. I suffered through the burning sting from the medicines going in my eye. I would eat an edible to calm my body, to calm my mind and fall asleep.

My body was pummeled. It could no longer keep up with the reality I was living. My body was resisting. Healing was happening much slower than I wanted it to. I had endured pain on all levels, physical, mental, spiritual. I was grasping at the old story. Looking for the old version of who I was. I had a long health journey ahead – sixteen months, I was in and out of eye surgeries that would take me out of commission for a few weeks. Each time I underwent a laser surgery, or needle in my pupil or surgery, my reality would completely alter. I would play and replay past occurrences, events, conversations. Even though I was still unable to see from my physical eye, I was being shown. My body could not resist the trauma and pain of the old story of who I had become. I could not stop holding on to the ideas of who I was, and my part in this crisis. My body had to catch up.

I was differentiating emotions from feelings. The emotions created physical symptoms, and I felt them trapped in my body. My nervous system was insanely distressed. There were so many feelings in my body that I didn't have words for. I sank deeper into my feelings. I was seeing what I had not allowed myself to feel. All the stories in my head how I became what I was. I had new eyes to see. I was able to simply see it all. See it for what it was. I was able to witness, view, observe, and feel my own self. All my emotions, habits, thoughts, behaviors, experiences. Why? Why did I believe he had all the answers? *Why am I* ignoring myself? I was in denial for so long. Everything I did not want to see, my own destructive behavior, my own relationship that I cherished. I sat with my true self, and I looked at everything I did not want to sit with and it. All I did was see.

I had very little energy. I soothed myself between these deep sessions of awareness with yoga breathing techniques and mantra meditation. When I was struck with a bolt of pain, a wave of immense sadness – I sat in that awareness and I recognized all that I was feeling, whatever it was in that moment. Sadness, anger, grief, pain, betrayal, rage, confusion – each feeling traveled over and consumed me. I would place one hand over my heart, one over my belly and would breathe in as much air as I could, feel the sensation, and exhale slowly. My body would calm, my thoughts would slow down, but I was drowning in self loathing. All the ugly, all the shame. I felt it deeply. With each breath in I would say my name to myself "Mila Guerrerra", with each breath out I would say "Remember who are." I would repeat it, and give thanks, for the things I had in the moment. My pillow, my comfortable bed, reminding myself things could be worse. I would fall into a sleep state and come back to the same place. When I showered, I would intentionally take the opportunity as another way to visualize my recovery. I would step under the hot shower, and I would ask for the water to wash the sickness, the sadness off of my body. My old Catholic roots were still present. The prayers, saints and guides. I used the old fashioned seven day candles that I remember my little Puerto Rican Abuela would light when she was praying for something. A tall slender candle with the Virgin Mary or ArchAngel Michael decorating the front of the candle with their prayer on the back. This became my practice. My ritual for every time I needed healing. I was learning to be gentle with myself. It seemed so foreign.

Your body speaks its own language, and sometimes sickness forces you to slow down. Being sick is hard enough. Being unwell makes life even harder. It makes hope a struggle. The chronic health issue I was rehabilitating through – made living my life even harder as I was thinking of my future. Caring for my delicate spirit was imperative. I had to breathe life back into my soul. I was learning to listen to all the messages my sickness was telling me. For me, it was the energetic experience that I was feeling in my body and putting myself back together. The way my body responded to what was happening to my life. I got very close to my guardian angels every day and every night.

Rick did not have emotional awareness or emotional regulation. He was incapable of recognizing that his fetish could have anything to do with my condition. He himself was wounded. I was living in a constant state of stress, repressed emotions which led to the breakdown of my physical and mental health. My body had not felt safe around my own husband for so long. It caused me to quiet down and shrink. I was afraid to speak my truth, he always shut me down. After so many years of holding so much energy, I was afraid of what his reaction would be? *Will he acknowledge the mess our marriage was in? Would he stop to hug me and tell me he loves me?* I hoped, I prayed, I wished he would. But deep down, I knew it would not be the response I hoped for.

Chapter Ten

I had to be slowed down. Had I not been forced to rest, *What would have become of me?* It was a state of isolation that was divinely timed. It created a safe hermit like space. In a strange way, it felt purposeful. It forced me to be with all the memories and feelings that I didn't want to talk about – but needed to be dealt with.

I was weak, I was traumatized, I was dazed. I didn't know what to do with everything I was processing. I was feeling sad, intense emotions, not always knowing where the feelings were coming from and why I was feeling everything so intensely. I was already highly sensitive, everything amplified one million percent. My reality was frightening.

Our relationship had already changed. Rick and I were drifting further apart. We didn't even kiss anymore, to say hello or goodbye. We didn't laugh together. It was a lonely place. But I became more observant. He did seem different. I still held space for him. I still loved him. He didn't have the emotional tools to understand.

I thought about myself.

Who am I, as a woman, wife, mother, daughter, sister and friend. Why am I here? Why is this happening to me? What is this trying to teach me? Is it about sex? Sex, without all the distortion and kinks. The attraction that we started with, before children, before marriage. Who was that version of me? When he loved me unconditionally. I was beautiful, and sexy just the way I was. That was the true essence of who I was. *When did I become this sad, sick weak shell of a woman? How did I become this?* I would think to myself, *I am his wife.* What happened to *"to have and hold and cherish?"* I had three children with *you. My body was their home. I loved them before I even held them.*

Was our relationship even real? *Am I that hard and complicated? Am I bitch?* I am a good woman, a good mother. I didn't ask for much, just his time, loyalty, love and commitment. Our marriage contract did not mean he owned my body. Marriage did not mean becoming a sex slave. I kept running back to him – because I was hoping love was still there for us. I missed him. But he was all that I knew. We were married for seventeen years. If I let him go, would I be able to breathe? I would have died just waiting for him to value me! All the love I had shown, all the times I put my heart on the line had not been received or wasn't returned. I hoped and prayed that he could look within himself.

During those months, I felt stuck in a place in my mind. I was seeing all the things, external distractions that pulled me from myself. I revisited all the times Rick told me he was just joking, I was being too sensitive. I was taking everything too seriously. I was being dramatic. I was blowing it out of proportion. This wasn't love. This wasn't a marriage. My life was more valuable than his sadistic enjoyment.

In this time, I could see the behavior that I was used to, and what I thought was normal. I began to see that it was induced. I could start to make sense of it in small pieces. It wasn't my true nature. It was imposed on me for so many years. It was this bombardment that I was hit with over and over again that was coming from his distorted mindset. That distortion always sounds normal. Like I should be going along with everything that he wanted. The realizations I was coming to. I was worthy and deserving of so much more. It was not who I was. When I thought I was connecting with my husband, I was actually disconnected from everything.

Who am I? Who am I being? I was constantly busy, distressed and ill-tempered. This wasn't me. This was the role I was playing. And it was totally real. But that other part of me – the part of me, that is absolute, was remembering who she was.

I was trying to rationalize my reality, still be a functioning mother, and figure out my life. My body could not resist the trauma and pain of who I was, who I had become. I was part of the problem and was figuring out my part in this crisis. I felt so conditioned to think I was overthinking, overreacting, being unreasonable. I had absorbed his thinking. I was looped into thoughts that led to the next loop. It took my whole marriage to figure out what were my beliefs, and what were his beliefs. Bombarded with thoughts. I surrendered deeply into all of my feelings. I couldn't understand all of my emotional output. I had an inability and fear of expressing my growing rage. Heavy waves of physical pain followed.

I had swallowed so many feelings. I had pushed my feelings so far deep, for so many years. Those feelings, they never go away. They just intensified.

There was no lying to myself anymore. I was becoming aware of all my core wounds that were stored deep in that shadow space. It was as if the darkness in my eyes was shining a spotlight. I was getting a better understanding of what needed healing. And I started to remember everything that I was. Everything that I was not, had to go to bring health and harmony. I was healing childhood issues, traumas, sadness, abandonment, lack, loss. I was processing through old. But – each time was different. I no longer felt the pain of those hurts. I just revisited it that time, that event, that thing I said, or that thing I didn't say. It was piecing together and processing old pain. I had judged myself for so long, I found I didn't need to anymore. I accepted and apologized to that version of myself.

One day, I woke from a nap. I could hear Rick in the shower. I felt his phone buzz on the other side of the night stand. He always had his phone on him. I took advantage of the few minutes that I had. He had already told me about Kayla from college and Anni from work. Conversations confirmed. I already knew it. But, there was another. Sarah. And her nipple. My old friend, ten plus years had passed since I had thought of her. Sarah and her nipple were on my husband's phone. I gasped. I set his phone down. I rolled across the bed to my side and curled up. I didn't say anything. I didn't do anything. My heart was already broken..

Heavy and toxic. It was a constant fog. I softened my own feelings of shame, sadness, weirdness, nervousness. Rick would never give me as many chances that I gave him. How many times did he think he could hurt me with the same bullshit? How did I miss his true nature?

During this period of isolation I pulled all my energy back. I had nothing to give. It was a period of unknown with major life changes ahead. Where I was in my journey, was exactly where I should be. I was being molded and shaped. As if my higher self needed to get me all alone, with no interference. To be changed from the inside out. The only way to get to know yourself and to get into alignment is to be one hundred percent honest about who you are, about your experiences and to love yourself anyway. Then, radical self acceptance. I learned everything I needed to learn about myself through isolation. It was a blessing in disguise

Certain emotions triggered me as I was clearing so many things. Things I thought I had already healed from. They were coming back to be readdressed. I realized I had to stop explaining myself to him. He was committed to misunderstanding me. I had to be slowed down, because I was aligned with him, and it was not a true reflection of who I was. I was overcompensating, overexplaining and over exerting my energy. He made me question every little thing about myself. My worth, my value, my truth. If you have to explain who you are over and over again, you are not with the right person. As confusing as it all was, it was leading me to my next version.

Because of the way my heart was created, I continued to forgive and give second chances and overlook certain behaviors. I know what it is like to be human and have flaws. But I also have morals and values and expected my husband to act like a husband. Everything came from such a low place within him. It had been dragging me down all along. He was holding me down in such a way that I was nearly completely diminished.

It is a humbling experience when you have to sit with the dysfunction you helped create.

Chapter Eleven

My health issue added more strain on the relationship. I was in and out of different specialists and doctors, causing unexpected financial constraints. I was dependent on Rick. We drifted further apart. We were in a disconnected space of resentment and burnout. I was holding on to this secret that was our marriage. I knew I had to tell him everything that I was feeling. The things that we didn't talk about. I didn't think he could handle my level of honesty. I didn't know how. I didn't have the words.

I had tried before, so many times. When I would articulate my thoughts, my voice became a whisper. Every time I would get a sentence out he would flip back on me or divert. He didn't want to hear anything I had to say. Rick had a way of covert mind games, word twists and manipulation, then joking and laughing. He would mix enough truth in with the lies that I questioned myself.

I could no longer ignore the state of our relationship. I knew I needed to talk to Rick about this. Why did I want to fix what was unfixable? I still had hope. I still wanted my family. I thought to myself, I am his wife, and I am struggling with something. Who else am I supposed to go to?

I meditated for courage. I prayed for courage. For courage I needed to stand in my conviction for my life. I was recovering from my ninth or tenth, who knows what eye surgery! I was resting on the couch. There was no way we could have this overdue discussion on our own. I had never been to therapy and the idea of it was scary. I knew I needed help. I asked him if he would go to marriage counseling with me. He is my husband. How could he not show up for me? Show me love and support? Rick said, "Yes."

I knew that I was not going to go back to who I was. The person Rick knew before, she was gone. There was nothing left of her. Rick let her go a long time ago. When he stopped paying attention to me, laughing with me, paying attention to my feelings, to the changes in my behavior. He made me feel like my presence was not important. I wasn't going to be stopped just because I was terrified. I had no idea how to move forward. *How was I going to tell him what I had to tell him? What was I going to tell him?* I spent the next week in a state of tension and angst. I wrote him a letter. A seven-page long letter. I wrote everything single I had been feeling.I had overwhelming and uncontrollable feelings of anxiety and anticipation leading up to our first couples counseling session.

I could barely breathe in the car on the drive to our first counseling session. The poor therapist! Her name was Carol, a warm, kind and conservative mid-fifties Christian family counselor. Introductions, formalities, family dynamics, etc. When it was my turn to speak, I went blank. I couldn't remember the words that I had written and rehearsed what I was going to say. I fumbled through my purse for my letter. I gulped. I called my guardian angels to be with me.

I read these exact words.

Dear Rick,

Thank you for coming with me here today. I know how difficult this is. I am scared. I am tired. I am exhausted. But I need to be heard. And I need to be acknowledged, I truly feel that you don't listen to me. You don't see me. This has caused frustration, agitation, so badly. The pain of everything manifested as a physical injury in my eye. I am sorry I got sick. I am sorry I burdened you. I am sorry I burdened our family. The frustration and insensitivity has been passed back and forth. When I talk to you I feel like you receive it as an attack. I know I upset you when I am upset. So I shut down. I let my voice go. Part of this injury. At the time I was sick. When I was suffering and in pain, I was all alone in literal darkness. I watched my life, I was able to deconstruct it. My whole life, my marriage, and I put it back together. I did this multiple times. I went deep.

Please know I wrote this out so I can communicate with you truthfully and express calmly what needs to be said. Because our situation is serious. It's almost vicious. I can't keep shifting back and forth between hard and harder. Being in this state of mind has kept me locked in a never ending book. I have to be able to heal and move forward physically. but mentally, I have been stuck in an angry, ugly place. I know, the past is the past and cannot change it. But my soul is broken, and I have to heal it.

The issues.

I didn't understand why HotWifing was your kink. I still don't. But you reduced me to garbage. I for real questioned in my darkest if you actually loved me. I wonder still. Because I replayed it, relived it, tried to reason with it. You were talking about sharing me as your fantasy back when we were twentysomething. I think to myself now WTF as realizations become clearer. I now feel like you were grooming me for this. At first the dirty talk was in the bedroom, I thought it was a turn on for fun because we were young and stupid. But I was the stupid one. Then we fast forward to having our kids phase, years later it's still a thing. Fine. I want to have an exciting bedroom life. I always did. The porn movies when we were younger, the sexy clothes and toys, all fine and good. But then you wanted more. The online chatting. You knew some were creepy and scary. So you found someone. You found me a man. You paraded me like a common whore. I fucked him. For you.

Then you wanted another man for me. Conversations online. Why am I talking to other men online flirting and sexting? Why aren't you flirting or sexting with me, your wife? Who are you flirting and sexting with? Do you remember all of the times, multiple times I would ask you why, why are you giving me away? You still can't tell me why. I found a man. Because you told me I should look around too. I met him three times.

Rick, what would you have done had I gotten murdered? Kidnapped? Raped? Tossed out of a car? Off a bridge? Pregnant? What would you have said? To my parents? To our kids? You would lie about it. Wouldn't you? You would say, you had no idea I was cheating, or some bullshit like that? How many other people have you shared my photos with? Did you post my pictures on websites? You just gave me away. Turned me into your whore. Used me afterwards for your own choreographed sex. And you never noticed me shrivel and shrink into sadness.

I am so angry at myself. I am disappointed in myself. Now I am lifting myself up. Our marriage is a shit show. I was so busy making sure that you loved me, that I never noticed that you weren't loving me. Right now I don't know that you ever did really love me. And here we are. We barely even talk to each other. I have tried to talk to you before. We have to look at our issues. I know they are ugly. I know they are hard.

We are raising our kids. We know better, We need to do better. We need to teach our kids to do better. It's our obligation to them. But we are failing them too.

I had to write these words just to be able to say them out loud. If I didn't share all these issues, the words would not have ever been said out loud. I know you have issues with me too. We are here. Can we see each other again? Because I can't keep barely surviving this marriage. We are in a crisis. We have to do better.

Thank you for listening.

I listed each of the women in the letter. My friend Sarah, her nipple on his phone. He knew what he was doing was wrong, the first time I caught him. Again, no remorse. My own handwriting on the letter was hard to read, because my feelings gushed into the pen and onto paper. I couldn't look up at him as I read. I don't think I would have been able to finish. I called him out on everything. It took everything inside me to speak the words and experiences from my entire marriage. I listed issues with the kids, parenting disagreements, core values and good choices. I could no longer not address the negative mindset and ripple effect it was taking. As I read the letter aloud, the more horrible my life sounded. If I looked at him I would freeze. I just kept reading, tears burning my cheeks.

I took a deep breath, and lifted my eyes from the pages I just read aloud. It was a truth bomb that had been ticking for so many years. I took another deep breath and a sigh of relief. Silence.

Rick looked at me, before he even uttered a word. His face. I already knew. In that moment, he was no longer the nice, charming guy, the admirable dad, the virtuous husband he portrayed himself to be. The truth exposed him. He took it as an attack. "I admit. It turned me on. I am sorry you feel that way."

The emotional hurt I felt in that moment is indescribable. Was I even breathing? Did he comprehend anything that I just said? Was that even an apology? Did he ever love me? Still more silence. I had no words. I could only imagine what Carol's face looked like. She began speaking to diffuse the situation before it could possibly turn any worse. Everything felt heated and rushed, my blood pressure was rising. It took a moment for me to hear what she was saying. "Rick, She's telling you now." Carol recommended each of us visiting with her separately, each week, and then together. We scheduled our appointments. We left. We drove home in silence. I don't think we spoke to each other for a couple of days.

I scheduled with Carol as soon as I could. I was not able to move forward. I was so tired of living at rock bottom. I was tired of being miserable and hating myself. And frankly, I didn't want to end up dead! My children were the only hope I had left. During that period of recovery, my children were my only reason for living. I was never going to compromise myself again. And I never wanted my kids to ever be in a position where they would compromise themselves. I didn't want my kids to attract a similar type of relationship and think it was okay.

After one of Rick's first session's alone with our new therapist, he surprised me when he asked me for a copy of the letter I wrote him during our very first session. I asked him why he wanted it. It was an assignment from Carol. He wanted to read it again. I told him I would get him a copy of it. I thought to myself, *Oh my gosh! This is a good thing! Progress.*

I was hopeful our couples sessions would ease the tension and anger. The hour began cordially. Rick was good at disguising his emotions. Sessions would become angry, argumentative. Sometimes it felt like we were fighting for our lives in therapy. The rift between us began to grow bigger. The tension became more evident in our home with our kids. We were straight forward with them. We told them we were working on our relationship in marriage counseling. As teenagers are, they looked up briefly, nodded while looking up from their phones. The kids were living their teen lives, school, studying, friends and football games and rules being tested.

As parents, we could not agree on discipline. We each took our side, and what began as an issue between the parent and child, became a problem between me and Rick. Kids know when parents aren't unified. They knew I was the strict parent and Rick lenient. Parenting became a hot topic in our counseling sessions. Coming up with a plan to set rules and help our kids make good choices became a battle to win for Rick. When one child would push boundaries, clothing choices, not checking in, curfew, Rick would respond with "I don't have a problem with it." or "I turned out just fine." His expression as if it were his inner sixteen year old speaking. Sometimes it felt as though he was favoring one of our kids, because their personalities were similar.

One of our kids was clearly falling into depression. I felt something was deeply wrong. I noticed my middle child not wanting to do anything. Hardly coming out of the bedroom. Barely eating. I knew the signs. Rick knew the signs. Grades dropping, little to no conversations. Responses were short, "Yes" or "No" or sometimes a look or grunt. I would bring it to Rick's attention. I would ask him if he had checked in or if he noticed a change in behavior. If there was something Rick didn't want to look at, or wasn't convenient for him, it simply would not exist for him. Rick would respond with "Middle child is fine. When we are together, we laugh and joke. It's when you are around. You are making it difficult because you aren't giving enough space."

My body instantly responded shooting back with the same venom to Rick, "That's what depressed people do. They get up, they show you enough of what you need to convince you that they are okay, then they close the door and hide away until they have to do it again tomorrow." Rick didn't get it. Or rather he did get it, he just didn't care or have the capacity to cope.

The issues were deep. Rather than co-parent for the kid's sake, it was easier to create more havoc. The seriousness of the circumstances would push me beyond my limit and capacity to cope. While it is not okay to yell, scream and rage like a crazy person, Rick would push me to that point. The sensitivity of the situation, the invalidation, the passive aggressive bullshit, the manipulation with a dash of smugness. He was creating chaos and he was enjoying watching my reaction. *This is my child we are talking about. How the hell could he act like that?*

Starting therapy was supposed to help us. Sometimes after therapy I felt worse and Rick felt worse, worse than when we started! When we began, it was painfully embarrassing and difficult. I felt like I was drowning. I felt even lonelier and more afraid. Therapy created an even bigger awareness of my thoughts of what was going on in my life. I felt beat up, beat down after sessions. There was an aftermath of post therapy fatigue and body aches. My depression was not going away. At Carol's recommendation, I sought more help. I had never been on medication before, but I took the next big step. I visited with a psychologist and started a regimen of medication to ease my depression symptoms and take better control of my mental health.

I left my part-time office job. I continually needed to take time off to accommodate for my health condition-it made sense for me to slow down. I began teaching a few yoga classes a week and committed myself to healing. I was trying to make sense of my life. For the first time, I was tending to my whole self – physically, mentally and spiritually. I met with Carol weekly, therapy provided a safe space and I knew I would benefit from it eventually. I read as much as I could – relationships, communication, parenting, I looked for other HotWifing stories like mine. I was trying to be the best mother I could be.

It had been so long since I felt remotely human. I was relearning. And I was applying new ways of being. My depression was showing me that my soul needed nourishment. I learned that my anger was a boundary – it was telling me that my basic needs were being ignored. My self-loathing and shame needed acceptance and love. My physical condition and exhaustion was a result of overstim-ulation and over functioning. I was recognizing the trauma living in my body.

My healing journey was the best commitment I ever made to myself. I still couldn't forgive myself but my thoughts were get-ting clearer. Therapy sessions would bring up all new issues to work through. My anger and frustration were only rising as we tried to dig deeper into our relationship through counseling. After a few months into counseling, Rick and I no longer drove together to our couple sessions. We drove in separate cars. I arrived and would be sitting in the room with Carol. Rick would arrive a few minutes later. Then the next time would be ten minutes later. He wasn't putting effort into our sessions. We no longer sat next to each other on the couch in her office. We sat separately from one another. We grew even fur-ther apart. Rick didn't take to counseling the way I hoped. He used personal sessions to discuss politics, work. Everything but our failing marriage. I started to see him morph before my eyes. He didn't want to acknowledge anything or even try. I found myself thinking, *Who is this person? Do I even like him? Does he even like me?*

The distance between us in our own home was emotionally charged and complex. He couldn't fully see me or understand me. Rick was literally running away from me. Yet, I was clinging while he was pushing me away. He wasn't running from me, he was running from himself. He abandoned our connection. But ended up aban-doning himself in the process. He lacked a healthy relationship with himself. Rick was always seeking out shallow, fake connections. His is porn additions created a lack of depth in our marriage. He kept pushing me away because he couldn't figure me out. He couldn't apply his logic to our situation. It was as if he was speeding up towards divorce. *Would he really rather lose me, than be honest about what he has done to me and what is becoming of our relationship?*

Rick was choosing to misunderstand me. He did not want to know the new person I was becoming. He was holding on to the old version of me. Expressing myself was futile when he simply wasn't capable of understanding. I was severely mishandled and I could not remember what it felt like to be safe to be myself in this stage of my life.

I was dedicated to my growth. I didn't care how it looked from the outside looking in. Who I used to be is no longer who I am. Could he, would he, accept that I was different?

Chapter Twelve

Mother's are always there to help. My mother lived nearby, about an hour away. Even though we had a good relationship, I would push away. She always held Rick in high regard. During my eye injury rehabilitation, she drove me to several doctor's appointments when Rick was unable to. My mother knew we were struggling in our marriage. She wanted to know how she could help. She had been watching me deteriorate for so long. I knew she was scared for me, I knew she was praying for me. But I kept my situation completely private. She had no idea how dysfunctional and toxic my true life was. I was too ashamed to tell her. She was trying so hard to help me, comfort me and support me. She knew I was beginning to crumble again.

Mom and I were at lunch one day when I received a text from my dear friend Marie. I immediately responded. Marie was beautiful, smart, stylish and funny. I felt like we had always been friends. Marie had a beautiful tattoo sleeve of blue butterflies. She wore a cute eyebrow piercing and her makeup was always flawless. Just like me, she was married with three kids. We had lots in common. Over the years, Marie had been to my home with her family for dinner and drinks. She was a part of one of my birthday celebrations. Marie was one of the realest women I knew. We really got each other. Her husband's job eventually relocated them about four hours away. We stayed in contact over the years through social media. But she had gotten sick. I was checking on her every couple of days after having tests to determine what was going on. She was diagnosed with a rare and aggressive cancer. There was no cure. I had been texting with her everyday, to check on her and cheer her up. After multiple surgeries, radiation, different treatments she was growing weaker, with no signs of improvement. She knew her time was coming. I was so sad for her and her family.

I broke down to tears at lunch. Marie wasn't even forty-five. I could not fathom what she and her family were going through. Without hesitating, my mom planned a road trip. We packed for a short weekend trip, just she and I. My eye situation was still an issue. Intense sunlight made me extra sensitive and I couldn't see very well at night. I discussed it with Rick. He knew I had remained in contact with her over the years, and that she was sick. He understood how important it was to me. I made arrangements with Rick for the weekend to hold down the house with the kids.

Mom and I were on the road the next weekend. It was so nice to share time in the car. It was peaceful. I was safe with my mom, in a way I had not felt in so long. She didn't ask questions. We just drove listening to music, we sang, we laughed and chatted along the way. I had no idea how badly I needed this get away, to clear my own thoughts. The change of scenery was good.

We arrived in the evening, settled. A late dinner at a local restaurant and grabbed a bottle of wine for the hotel room. I texted with Marie. I made arrangements to visit with her at her home the next day. I stopped on the way to buy a plant, candy and tea. I prepared myself mentally and emotionally to be with my beautiful friend who l loved so much.

It had been three or four years since we had seen each other. Her husband Josh answered the door, we hugged in hello. I could see he was sincerely happy that I made the trip. Marie was resting on the couch. She sat up from her pillows and beamed a smile so big at me! She was connected to a monitor with wires and a machine pumping her full of medicine. I hugged her bones. I pressed my heart on her heart and I held her tight. She looked so frail. I did really well, I didn't cry but I wanted to squeeze her so hard. I was scared I would break her though. Her head was covered in a wrap. I sat close to her on the couch, just in awe of her. Our visit was short and beautiful. She tired quickly from the excitement and the laughs. I hugged her again. I prayed silently while I embraced and held her close. I told her I loved her. I hugged Josh. I knew it was the last time I would see my Marie. She fought a good battle for two more months. I am so thankful for the friendship and the time I shared with Marie.

Mom and I still had the rest of the day, and the next to share time. We were both exhausted from the emotional visit we just had. Marie recommended her favorite restaurant and dinner. Mom and I shared a wonderful dinner and toasted Marie. We returned to our hotel room, and sat by the pool for the rest of the evening. My heart was heavy. My thoughts were heavier. I missed my kids and I was overwhelmed with sadness. I could feel my mom's eye's, observing me the entire time. "What's going on Mila? I can see that you are not okay. What's happening? How can I help you?"

I felt small, powerless, voiceless over my life for so long. *Could I even muster the words?* But if I didn't say anything, if I didn't ask for help, I couldn't lie to myself any longer. If I died tomorrow, no one would know what really happened. If I did not say what was wrong, I was never going to survive my marriage. I was going to end up dead. I sat up tall in my chair. I tried to clear my throat, I was searching for words, I had no idea what to say. We sat across from one another in intense silence. Mom could tell. She knew I had something big to say. And she was going to wait patiently and kindly, for me to find the words, my voice to say it out loud. I tried to get words out. I stopped myself. I tried again. *What words could I say to my own mother about my biggest mistake?*

I swallowed my pride. I took a very big sip of wine. I got a little taller in my seat and gave her my full attention. I said, "Mom, I want you first to take a moment, take a breath, call your angels, say a prayer and protect your energy. This is mine, and I don't want you to feel any of what I am feeling. I'm asking for protection and words to say this."

My mom was a strong, faithful, sensitive woman. I knew the sting of what I was about to say would be a dagger in her heart. I looked into her eyes, I said "Mom, I want you to know I am okay." I repeated, "I am okay. I promise. This is the hardest thing to say out loud to you. Again, I am okay." She nodded at me and told me she loved me. I told her I loved her. I breathed in, I said, "I am sorry for the words that I am about to say." In my strongest whisper, I said to her, "Rick has a sexual fetish. It's called HotWifing. The man gets pleasure from knowing his wife, sleeping with other men, then having sex with her. I did this for him with three men."

Immediately, I could see, I could feel her heart split in half. My mother's face transformed. Her eyes widened, she just stared, unmoving, unblinking in shock. I said it again, "I am okay. But it's destroying me." I stopped talking. I knew that she was overwhelmed with emotions that she didn't understand and didn't know how to respond. I could see her processing, emotionally unable to move like nothing around her was real.

I could feel tightness in my throat, tightness in my chest, my heart pounding, but I couldn't express any emotion. I looked at her, I leaned in a little closer. I said again, "I am okay. I am sorry. I'm so sorry." I could see she was wrapping her mind around the entire situation.

She said, "What are you going to do?" I responded, "I have to get out. I need an army."

It was the first time I had said those words out loud. We sat outside late into the night. I drank more wine. It was one of the hardest conversations I ever had. She asked questions – When? Why? How? I was doing my best to answer her questions, without answering her questions. I was stuck in a pattern, constantly preoccupied with concealing my secret life for so long. I was still recovering from the eye situation, and I had just visited with my dear friend for the very last time. I was flooded with anguish, shame and now guilt. I was in the worst time and space of my life. I had done such self harm and judged myself as a bad person.

I didn't want to hurt or burden my mother, I was forty-seven years old so I didn't want to make her responsible for my life. But I was fragile. We talked all night. My mother, an emotional and passionate woman went through extreme feelings of wanting to mother me, protect me, hold me, to the opposite end of the spectrum, a violent rage and anger toward Rick and his abuse. I fell asleep in my mom's bed that night. It was the most peaceful sleep I had in months. The impact of secrets is isolating, destructive and detrimental.

We headed home the next day. I could feel my mother's shock and sadness on our drive home. My heart was splitting open. Again, I assured her – I was okay. I was working on healing in every capacity. I shared so much from my heart. I told my mother, I felt her prayers over me many times when I was sick. When I felt like I wanted to give up on everything. The realization that I was disposable to my husband almost killed me. I knew I couldn't die, because Rick would have just lied to her. He would have lied to everyone.

We cried, we prayed. I knew I had to give thanks for this injury. Because it did give me new eyes to see myself, to see my life. Even though I didn't know what that life was supposed to be anymore.

Chapter Thirteen

I was feeling extreme shell shock from my trip, but I was happy to be home, to be in my personal space, hug my children, soak in my tub, and sleep in my own bed. I had much to think about. Rick knew I was heartbroken when I returned from visiting Marie. He hugged me. It was a quiet evening and we were actually sitting together with some evening television. The kids were upstairs, and the night was just what I needed. A peaceful evening at home – with wine of course. He was making an effort. And I reciprocated. The evening included some playtime with our pets, something that we hadn't done together in such a long time. We ended up having a silly photoshoot with our dogs. Being with Rick like this was familiar and sweet. We were laughing together and in that moment, it felt good in my heart.

Later in the evening, Rick was sitting on the edge of the couch, scrolling through the photos he had taken. I smiled and leaned in closer to admire the pictures. As he swiped his phone to the left, we giggled at our goofy dogs. There was a picture of our two dogs, with bright overlaid text "Happy Birthday from My Pups-" With curiosity,

I said "Oh – who's birthday is it?" He paused. He stammered. His shoulders dropped. It's my friend Anni from work.

I didn't say a word. His inner demon was out, and it was front and center. *What in the actual hell is wrong with him?!!* I thought to myself as I got up, filled my glass of wine to the top, and went out the back door. I just stood there on my back porch. I had not yet fully processed my conversation with my mom from the trip. I had just arrived home four hours ago. *And my PIECE OF SHIT husband was fucking sending pictures of OUR DOGS to some stupid bitch out of state that was his co-worker with fake tits? Right in front of me.* My dogs are like my children. A controlled fury began to brew in me. I paced up and down my back porch. *Did he send pictures of our kids too? What did she know about me?*

I don't know how much time had passed when Rick walked outside all puffed up, because no one gets angrier than a person when they are caught. He was ready for confrontation. "What, I can't wish a friend a happy birthday?" *Did he actually believe his own bullshit? Did he think he could still act like this and be a good person?*

This was his tactic. Rather than admit being caught, AGAIN, because he would never acknowledge what he was doing was wrong. Rick would use my reaction to reverse the issue and tell me I was out of control.

What Rick didn't know was I read his texts while he was in the shower. An opportunity that I took full advantage of when I was recovering just a few weeks before. I saw the conversation that he and Anni were having. She created her own account on the same adult website that Rick and I used to be connected on. I knew her account name. They had probably been there for months. *Fucker!!!* I was pissed. My voice whispered, because I was trying to control my rage, I looked at Rick and said, "Next time send her your dick pic over the website. Oh, but you probably already did." I yelled at him, "Don't send pictures of our dogs to your side piece." I silenced him. He turned around, walked in the house.

I followed him in, and I said "Rick, don't even think about coming into the bedroom." The idea of being in the same room with him revolted me. I wanted to knock him over the head. Punch in the throat. Stomp his balls. I wanted to run him over repeatedly.

Did he think I was going to keep doing this forever? Did he actually expect me to be able to keep the peace, ignore his behavior and tolerate his bullshit? Again? AGAIN? He could neglect me and ignore me in our house, but I can't complain about it? How much did he think I would take?

There was never going to be peace in our home. Rick only gave me mayhem. And I was mirroring it back. Rick could never understand that the hurt was so deep, it penetrated my core. A soul wound. He didn't care about anything but himself. I was beyond broken. He was never going to change. He didn't want to. He wouldn't acknowledge HotWifing was what damaged and destroyed our family. I was tired of fighting for what I loved. It didn't want to be fought for. I was tired of hurting and being hurt. I gave up hope he would change, that our marriage would improve, that we could grow old together. I gave up on the illusion of our marriage. It wasn't even real. That was the worst part. Our entire story was a lie. All the answers I was seeking were doing nothing but cause me more pain. Why was there so much drama? So much intrigue? *Why is he pretending to work on our relationship? Why did he hug me when I walked in the door, then act like it was my fault that I caught him?* Why did I need these answers?

I gave up. There was no restoring my trust. He had a pattern and was unwilling to change. And I was unwilling to tolerate this cycle of destruction any further. It was easier for Rick to play these games, rather than be honest with himself about what he had done.

I was seething all night long. Betrayal, anger, rage, confusion, sadness, frustration, wrath, everything amplified all at once. *He thinks he's never to blame for anything. He thinks he's always right!* I was having every "Oh, hell no" moment with each replay. I was standing up for myself by calling out his behavior. He lied, denied and deflected. Made me question my feelings and facts, my sanity. Consistently keeping me enslaved. He planted so many seeds of doubt in me, disguised as concerns for me, my health.

My anger was essential in this decision. I went to this magical place of *Fuck This Shit, Fuck You, I Deserve Better!* I was no longer going to explain myself over and over again. Our marriage no longer benefited him. As soon as I put a demand on our marriage, he detached. There was nothing left to talk about.

My rage would subside long enough for the fear to make its appearance. Everything was so big, so heavy, so present. It was taking over my body. This was the person who was supposed to love me forever. My husband! I was dying inside. Divorce is already hard. I could not imagine divorce in my dysfunctional situation? I didn't know where to begin. My kids! I didn't have any money. My kids! I didn't have a full-time income. My kids! I was still healing from the trauma of my chronic eye condition. If he hurt me this badly, was he capable of harming our kids too? I didn't sleep that night. That night was torture, one of the worst nights of my life.

Life as I knew it before was over. I had to think. I had to strategize. I didn't know who he was. No one was coming to save me.

It was up to me to dig deep and develop courage and claim my life back. Most of my battles were fought alone with my own fears and judgements. The hardest thing I had to do was be a mom, while I had to fight tooth and nail to remember who I was to free myself from my husband.

I emailed Carol late in the night. I told her the events that transpired over the weekend. That I confided and told my mother everything. And that I caught Rick having his online fun, right in front of me. That asshole. I told her I didn't want to be married. I didn't know how I was going to move forward, but I was done.

Our upcoming appointment with our therapist was in three days. I couldn't stand the sight of him! I didn't have a plan or any idea what to plan for. I didn't know what version of Rick was going to show up. How was he going to flip it back on me, in the way that he was so cunning at. He wouldn't own his feelings, he would project them on me and spin me out causing me to justify and defend myself. He was never going to apologize. Our house felt like a minefield, those days leading to our appointment. I spent the next three days in a state of numbness.

The night before our therapy session, he entered our bedroom and went to his side of the bed. I paused. *Is he actually getting into the bed to go to sleep? In OUR bed? What in the hell is going on?* He had spent two nights sleeping on the pull out couch in his office. He was acting as if nothing had happened. As if everything was normal. Did he actually perceive himself as innocent? The audacity. I wasn't turning the other cheek. *Who the fuck did he think I was? I'm not his mother!*

I looked at him and said, "Rick, you are not sleeping anywhere near me." He looked at me with contempt and said, "Crazy bitch."

That's when he began to label me as crazy. I slept with the door to my bedroom locked for the remainder of our time in that house.

I arrived at Carol's office and sat in my usual spot. My memory of the appointment is grainy. Our emotions were already heightened. Tension was high. Voices were higher. Rick could only see our marriage from his vantage point. He felt entitled to anything he wanted, regardless of how it affected anyone else. He disregarded everyone's feelings in our family for some instant gratification with random women. He could only speak and see what was in best interest. There was no respect, conclusion, or resolution in that session.

Rick had no idea how to act during conflict. He could pretend to deny it. To make himself feel better about getting caught, getting exposed, or hearing the truth. But it didn't matter. He couldn't deal with it. He refused any accountability or responsibility, as he did in every other situation. Instead of owning a mistake or owning his own issues, he would conveniently forget something happened. He was going to try to re-write and reframe everything! In order for Rick to be honest with me, he would have to be honest with himself. He was not capable.

Chapter Fourteen

My marriage was over. I had no clue where to begin. Staying in my marriage was comfortable and stable. I could no longer endure living like this any longer. I wasn't one hundred percent healed from my eye condition. *How do I start a divorce right under Rick's nose?* I had no money of my own. I was a stay-at-home-mom for years, and when I did work it was a part-time or low wage job. Rick was the breadwinner. How was I going to afford it? How was I going to support myself and my kids? My kids were what I was most worried about; I didn't want to cause any further damage. I didn't want to ruin their lives too. This was not a normal divorce. Everything was of an adult nature, and I was mortified. I could no longer allow myself to live in this condition. Part of me was saying *Suck it up and get divorced!* The thought of having to go to court, and deal with more conflict made me paralyzed with anxiety. I refused to look back on my life with any regret.

Fighting the fear was not easy – it was a daily battle. I had the determination, perseverance and superhuman courage. I had only confided in my mother. When we were on our road trip home, she offered help. But there was one more thing I had to do. I had to ask my stepfather for help. My stepfather – Miguel had been in my life since I was ten years old. I was a pain-in-his-ass teenager, but he loved me like his own. As promised, my mom kept everything I shared with her private. Miguel knew. Something was seriously wrong. When mom returned home and he inquired what was going on, all she could bring herself to say was that Rick was not the person we thought he was.

Miguel, a prideful Latin man, always gave the impression that he was serious, professional and strict. He worked hard for his wife and four kids. Miguel taught us the values of family, loyalty, and respect. He was very active in providing support and protection to his family. He gave us reassurance, discipline, emotional and spiritual leadership, and so much love. Telling Miguel I needed his help to divorce Rick under these circumstances was incredibly difficult. This wasn't ordinary bad news. I was his child. He raised me better than this. The shame I was feeling, the thought of his reaction kept me in knots until we met. There was no going back.

We had to coordinate schedules, meeting in private. I had a short window of time. We met at a little restaurant. Ironically, it resembled the type of place that people go when they don't want to be recognized. Miguel is truly a powerhouse of a man. He was composed. Voice got a little gruff. He said, "Okay. I will pray for Rick." At that moment, I didn't know what to say. I don't think I said anything at all. In my head, I remember thinking to myself *You're gonna pray for him?* The child in me was screaming inside for her dad to beat him up, but I thanked him. I hugged him. I said, "I am sorry for everything." I am forever thankful. The impact of what I shared was a lot. I didn't hear from him for over a week. I was devastated. I knew he was processing his thoughts, processing his anger. He saved my life.

I navigated my routine carefully. Researching divorce processes, reading about lawyers where and when I could get privacy. Many times I would pull over into a parking lot or park to make or return calls. The next few weeks began to feel like we were all walking on eggshells. Nothing was ever just a simple question, a statement or conversation. There were mixed messages, passive aggressive comments, and projections. We were living in a battle zone.

Everything in our family grew more toxic by the day. I noticed a strange behavior – Rick would mouth words I couldn't decipher to the kids, or make a face, shake his head in disagreement while we were trying to have a discussion. *Does he think I don't notice?* It was impossible to argue with someone who won't listen. Rick acted as if everything that was happening was my fault. He put us in this position.

Rick knew all the buttons to push. There was an aggression that seemed unwarranted. His mind games continued and would again push me beyond my limits, beyond control where I would literally lose my mind. He was strategic. He moved dirty. I was in a fog, feeling guilty for having a reaction to his abusive behavior. I became hyper vigilant to everything around me. Why couldn't I control myself? Because, we never got to any real issues, truth made him so uncomfortable. I could not believe the vicious side. He would respond with, "Yeah, okay, whatever." He used specific tactics to deter me. Saying things, trying to change my mood, get into my head. He did everything to keep the focus away from the root causes and emphasize my reaction. He painted me as self centered, unpredictable, unstable. He liked doing whatever he wanted, didn't care who he hurt, but he didn't like being held accountable. Rick didn't want any more truth to come out. He was committed to concealing it.

Raising kids is hard enough – especially during the teen years, when they are naturally testing boundaries, learning themselves, making new friends and relationships and responsibilities. It's such an important time. Naturally – behavior can get a little rebellious during these years. But something began to feel different. I began to notice a change in their behavior. The kids stopped responding to my texts, weren't completing simple chores, and shot more attitude than normal. I would ask Rick, "Have you heard from the oldest child? I messaged and haven't heard back." To which he would tell me, "Oh, the oldest child asked me about attending an event and I said yes. He claimed he thought I was informed. No. That was news to me.

This became a regular occurrence. There were several situations, with all the kids that occurred at different times, different issues. Some were very serious situations. Rick and I would argue. His response was always weak, "I told them to tell you." Conversations began to get more heated. He seemed to be running interference between me and the kids. It became angrier and more aggressive. If I ever tried to point out anything, he became very triggered and would shut down. It became subtly more ruthless a little more each day. Consequences weren't part of Rick's dynamic. He could perpetrate these behaviors and get away with it. *Bastard.*

There was so much misery. Rick was stuck and stubborn in his ways. He still devoted his time to the wrong things, the wrong people. Again, I was feeling misunderstood no matter what I said or did. Rick was sending a clear message. I was not welcome. He was constantly trying to eject me out of situations. Even the simplest tasks became obstacles. It was horrendous. We were both in two completely different head spaces, heading in opposite directions. And I took the bait.

There were so many moments. I constantly felt like something was wrong with me. *Who am I? Where am I going? Which way is up? Which way is down?* Dust and debris everywhere. I lived it so long. There was so much to lose. My relationships with my kids, it meant everything. It was the only thing that mattered to me. His behavior became more dreadful, once even going as far as sabotaging a holiday weekend. The level of immaturity was staggering.

The way you speak to your wife shows how you love her. It sets the tone of how children speak to their mother. A husband and wife are supposed to be partners. My kids were demonstrating the same behavior Rick was showing me. He allowed them to do the same things he did. Staying in their rooms. Staying up late. Not checking in when out with friends. Ignoring. Talking back. No respect. A deep sadness formed in my heart. This was not the foundation I had created.

Children depend on both parents to regulate their lives. How could he claim to love his children when he deliberately acts to destroy their mother? That is not love. *By disrespecting me did he think that he was doing the right thing? Could he not see he was disrespecting us all? Did he forget what our values were? Did he have any values left?* I didn't know what to do. It stung so deeply. They witnessed their dad talking down to me. Intentionally giving me his back. Silent treatment. Sneaking around. He allowed them to treat me, the way he treated me. And he had no problem with this behavior. Children are not leverage. I was done being nice. I had been ignored, repeated myself till I was blue in the face, now I was enraged. How could I not be?

Everything I said regarding parenting our kids was lost in translation. I didn't just snap one day and decide to be a crazy wife to him. The situation had gotten to a point where nothing was registering with him. Yes, the words you choose matter. Your tone matters. Your words have power. I made my share of mistakes. Huge ones. This life doesn't come with a handbook. And certainly not one for these circumstances. I still ask my adult children for forgiveness from time to time.

Rick was watching me go through this journey, constantly dropping seeds of doubt. He had to put me down, to raise himself up. In order for him to be more, he had to make me less. He had to take away, so he could have more. He always was pushing to make me smaller. I began to detest him more and more every passing day. He watched me crawl out of the dark things that he created to destroy me.

Somewhere deep down I know, Rick knew he was not treating me properly. We had so much history. We had an even bigger trauma bond. He once had a beautiful heart. He knew he made a huge mess. He experienced true happiness with me, but wanted to go back and forth. We shared so much together. I gave him peace. A home and a family. I provided a lot for him emotionally, spiritually and energetically, more than he realized. These are things Rick never learned to value. I instilled a level of confidence in him. But he only saw the world at face value. Still unable to connect with the deeper part of himself. Part of me prayed for God to show him how he was acting. The other part of me wanted to stab him. The Rick that I met, vs the Rick that was in front of me. It put me in a difficult place. *The version that drew me to him, who was he? Where did he go? Did he really ever exist?* There was something that literally switched.

Evolution was happening for me. I didn't understand how it was working through me, I had to trust it. I was being given the opportunity to change. The way I was thinking, acting and being. I was seeing myself in my thoughts, my actions, my emotions. Seeing it made me choose a new way to be. I could recognize my thoughts. See how I was acting. I had never felt this before.

My yoga and meditation practice is what brought me to a place of calm. It was my way of supporting myself to ease the weight of everything I was carrying on my shoulders. I would affirm to myself. I am aware that anxiety is rushing through me. I am aware that my heart is racing. I am aware that my thoughts are racing. I am aware of anger, sadness. I am aware that if I kill my husband I will go to jail. It would just let it rock and ravage out of me. Sometimes I would cry and feel sorry for myself. Sometimes I wanted to hire a hitman. Sometimes you just need your girlfriends, wine and a box of tissues.

Spending time with girlfriends was always important to me. I never needed an excuse to catch up with them – lunch, shopping and sharing time was part of who I was. Since becoming sick and beginning marriage counseling, I had not socialized and did not maintain my connections. I had many friends, but I avoided getting too close with most. Female friendships can be challenging, but they are so very important. Your female friendships are a compliment to who you are – your personality, your quirks, your weirdness. While I had a large circle of friends, there were only two girlfriends that were in my inner circle. And even they did not know everything.

The moment Theresa and I met, we were instant friends. She was a feisty Latina, with a big energy. Also married to a white man with three kids. We were so much alike. Over the years, Theresa and I shared lots of wine, food, family, music, dancing, holiday's, laughs, tears, problems, prayers. She was always my partner in crime and soul sister. She was street smart and book smart, accomplished in her career. One of the strongest women I have ever met. She is my person. Our friendship was always solid. Despite any times that we lagged in connecting because of work, family obligations, we were always able to pick up right where we left off, like no time had passed. Theresa was no stranger to loss. Both her parents were tragically killed early in her life. She was a strong survivor, passionate about her life, and her family. I admired Theresa's marriage to John. You can just tell with them as a couple, they were the real deal. John was a good husband and father, and they had a wonderful relationship.

Theresa knew me as well I knew myself. I shared with her that I was depressed, and that Rick and I were struggling in our marriage and been working our way through counseling. She poured the wine, I poured out my heart. She was kind and empathetic. As much as I loved and trusted Theresa, I still couldn't tell her my secret. She called to check on me a few weeks later – she caught me in an agitated state, I told her that I was about to meet with a divorce lawyer. She was stunned.

We planned to get together a couple of days later. Theresa arrived with food, booze and flowers, I opened the door, my eyes watered. Theresa is one the most generous people I have ever met in my entire life. She always gave with her heart. We settled down for a girl's night in. Once the wine kicked in, the emotion started to overflow. We were seated shoulder, probably on a second bottle of wine, when I started to share. Just as I told my mother a few weeks prior, I began delicately. Getting the words out of my mouth again was a struggle. "Theresa, first, I need to know that I'm okay." She sat, with her eyes wide open, and listened. With no judgment. She held my hand, leaned in closer to me, silent tears down her cheek as she listened to every word.

Theresa is one of those people that is never at a loss for words. She is intuitive, quick-witted, straight forward and steadfast. She had no problem getting in your face and telling you how it is, and how it's going to be. I loved her spirit and her passion. She was completely shocked. No words. In the months ahead she was my caregiver, protector, bartender, advisor and guardian angel. She wiped my tears, held my hand, fed me, got me drunk, gave me advice, prayed for me and with me.

I met Ruby at a Wednesday night yoga class. A beautiful Korean girl with a big, bold energy and a great vibe. She was about ten years younger than me and engaged to be married. I enjoyed chatting with her, but never thought we would become friends. We didn't have anything in common and I wasn't looking to add a new person into my life. We bumped into each other at the store after yoga one day and it was like she was my long-lost friend. Funny, at the moment I couldn't remember her name when we went to say goodbye. I accidently called her Theresa! She immediately gave that girlfriend look, "Bitch, what did you call me?" I laughed, I apologized, and told her Theresa is my best friend, and you have a strange sense of familiarity to me. We stood in the aisle for another thirty minutes to talk more. We exchanged phone numbers and were hanging out the next week.

I didn't know her as long as I knew Theresa, but the friendship was real. She was always up for an adventure, with a bit of a wild streak and a take no shit attitude. Her energy was a mix of zen and gangster. While we were hitting it off, I didn't want to let her in too close. We were still getting to know each other. And I didn't want her to know about my dysfunctional real life at home. But making friends as an adult is hard. We became closer, and I was so happy to have her in my life. She came over regularly for yoga and conversation. She had healing energy and was a fierce protector. I began to love and trust her. I hit another deep depression, and I confided in Ruby about my situation. "I fucking hate that misogynistic piece of shit rat face." After I told her, it was hard to have her over because she could not hide her anger. But I loved her for it. Sometimes when you are in a situation, at the time, you don't always realize how horrible it is, because it's too hard to handle.

There are friends, and there are people who become so much more than that. They are once in a lifetime people. The power of female friendship cannot be underestimated! Girlfriends are a source of joy, trust, comfort and support. They are cherished people that are precious and should be treasured. Theresa and Ruby are a huge part of my survival. I don't know how I would have survived without them. I am forever grateful.

I wasn't ready to move fast forward with the divorce process, but Rick's abuse and neglect were piling up. I had my tribe of women supporting me. I was careful and strategic. I was going to escape this.

Chapter Fifteen

Rick was a core part of who I was. Our connection was once powerful and beautiful. Or so I used to think. I was still coming to terms with deception, denial and betrayal. I was having a hard time with everything I was experiencing. *How am I supposed to handle it all? Where do I go from here? How do I recover from the shock of everything I've been through, what I am still going through.* I would fall back into a nostalgic pattern. We could have had such a beautiful life together. This was not how it was supposed to be. But I knew I couldn't reach him.

I had the support of my dearest friends, my siblings and my parents. I was breaking free. I still didn't have a plan, or money or a job, but I took the next big step. The biggest leap of faith I had ever taken in my life. I found a divorce lawyer that felt right for me. I scheduled my consultation. I could barely speak. I had my mother for support and she had her checkbook. My voice whispered again as I had to retell the secret of my marriage to another person. She walked me through the process, what to expect and how to move forward. I was frazzled by the sneaking around I was doing. I was listening to her, but was I really comprehending everything she was saying to me? I felt dizzy. My face felt heated. I was making these big life changing moves and decisions and I was scared to death.

My capacity was growing. I stopped questioning, I had to trust that I was supported and protected by my angels and ancestors. I filed for divorce. Without telling Rick. I was so overwhelmed from the meeting, I left without my documents. I was on my way home, I whooshed out of her office, so quickly. I didn't realize I left my newly filed divorce documents in the restroom. I was deep in the trenches. What I was going through was not pretty. It felt so messy. My plan was to serve Rick directly, face to face in our next counseling session with Carol. I was building my words, my mental and moral strength, to tell Rick I wanted a divorce. I wanted to end with dignity, respect and integrity. I wanted to make the process as easy as possible for our kids. I was choosing to heal and needed peace and hope for my future. It did not include him. Now I had to figure out my words carefully, prepare for his response, consider the kids and keep calm. Deep breaths. Affirmations. It was time to take action.

I was startled by a call from Rick. He never called me anymore. My heart stopped. *Did he see me as I was leaving the lawyer's office?* He was calling to tell me his parents would be in town for a few days. *Fuck! Fuck! Fuck!* I got a sinking feeling in the pit of my stomach. A feeling of dread that made me feel less than my usual self began to take over. Again, they scheduled a visit at the most inopportune time. And it happened to be a birthday weekend for my youngest. Was the universe against me? I wanted to bang my head against the wall. The soon to be ex-laws were actively house hunting in our area. I was doing my very best to just hold it together, this added another level of stress to an already intense week. They were already toxic to our relationship, to our household. I planned to do my very best to keep a low profile during their visit. I vowed to myself to keep my cool, this would be the last time I would ever be seeing them. I just had to make it through the weekend. I could do this. I lit a candle, prayed for grace, guidance and protection.

Luckily, they were busy most of the time. It only affirmed that them moving to our same state would cause even more strain on my already failing relationship. I knew I was making the right choices for my future. The entire family navigated the next couple of days as best as we could, Rick and I avoiding each other, but keeping up our charade as husband and wife. I felt like an imposter. We celebrated my youngest birthday as a family and made the time the best we could.

The in-laws had one more meeting before planning their road trip. We agreed to meet for a family dinner at our house, before they were to return to their home. Soon, I knew I could breathe a sigh of relief! I ran off to run my errands and prepare for the evening. I was almost through their visit. I could get back on track with my plan, to serve Rick with divorce papers at our counseling session.

While I was shopping for our "Last Supper," my phone rang, another call from Rick. "Where are you?" He knew I was running errands and what our plans were for the remainder of the day. "I am at the store, what's up?" I responded, not thinking anything unusual. Rick said, "My parents were in a car wreck." Silence. I instinctively stopped dead in my tracks, left my full basket, and immediately started to walk out of the store.

"Are they okay?" I asked, as I picked up my pace. I couldn't gauge anything at the moment, I was walking quickly to the exit. He said "They were rattled, but they're okay." They were able to drive their car and were on the way back to our house. I made my way to the house as quickly as I could. They were in their seventies, in pretty good health, but a car wreck is obviously no joke for anyone no matter how big or small.

I headed home and within minutes my in-law's arrived, looking visibly shaken. We gathered, grabbed some water and chatted. "Are you guys okay?" Rick and I both asked them. Edna seemed to still have tremors in her hands. I told her I think she should go to the ER, just to make sure. She still seemed a little flustered. Better to be safe. My father in-law seemed oblivious to her state. He was ranting and raving, still upset from the accident. Both Rick and I mentioned the emergency room again. *Shit!* Their return trip home was now delayed. Their car required immediate repairs to make the nine hour trip. My father in law slowed down enough to tell us what happened. Somehow they were cut off exiting the highway and spun off the exit ramp. They were very, very lucky. I asked about the other driver, "Are they okay? Were they carelessly texting? Did they have a seizure or heart attack?

No. None of the above. It was an accident. Luckily everyone was okay. Rick and I stood, listening, not quite knowing how to respond. Rick Sr. proceeded to tell the rest of the story. After the cars collided, they spun out, remarkably landing perfectly safe. It could have been worse – they easily could have flipped. He navigated his way across the busy exit lane between cars, to confront the other driver. He looked into the car and said to the driver, "You better have good insurance." Rick and I were both shocked to hear that immediately after being spun off the road, this seventy year old man was able to walk across traffic.

Both of us ignored the insurance comment. Rick Sr. continued, "That stupid Black bitch." The words rolled so comfortably off his tongue.

My shoulders dropped, my chin tilted down and my voice dropped. My past experience over the years with my in-laws racist comments flashed through my entire body, fire in my belly. I looked at him, my eyes glaring like my voice. "Do not talk that way in my house." I did not take my eyes off his ugly face. Dead silence.

The tension was palpable, "We should get you to the emergency room." Rick Sr. said to Edna – as they got up and walked out the door. Rick walked them out of the house. I watched them walk down to their busted car, my eyes staring daggers at them for what just occurred in my house. I wanted to scream. I could not blow it off. I could already hear Rick already defending the status quo, "They're just old, from another generation."

I was still fuming for the rest of the day and into the next. I couldn't let it go. My thoughts ruminating all night. Remembering, replaying all the previous times they revealed that ugly side. I was too uncomfortable to say anything in the past, and how unsettling it was not to ever speak up. It brought all those feelings back. Anger, embarrassment, stress, defensiveness, resentment. Ugh! All the times they used racial terminology, the Black cook, the Indian check out girl. In casual conversations, stories and experiences, race isn't a necessary part of a story. But if the person is white behind the counter, or the server is white, no one ever mentions it. In the past I was frozen in my tracks because I would think to myself, *Did my in-laws really just say that?* It's easy to get caught off guard when you hear a derogatory comment. It's so upsetting. I was always troubled by their hatred and arrogance. I was sick and tired of their blatant disrespect and hatred. *I am glad I said what I said! Fuck yeah I was.*

I always wished Rick would choose me when I had shared with him in the past how his parents' behavior made me feel. *Why the hell did I care?* I was telling Rick I was divorcing in the upcoming week. I didn't have to ever deal with them in this capacity again. I was so embarrassed and ashamed of myself for being a part of that family for almost twenty years. My kid's grandparents spoke like this. I was repulsed. *Good riddance!*

Everything was front and center. It was so clear that it was time to go. That spotlight again. I was looking at everything wrong in my life. These people were supposed to be my family. No. This was his family. They were important people to him. We came from two totally different backgrounds. Culturally, it felt as if the tallest mountain was between us. I don't know how Rick excused this behavior. I know he got push back from his family. It was how he was raised. It was a huge obstacle and problem during our entire marriage. I was beyond done. I needed Rick out of my life. I needed to focus on my divorce and my plan forward.

It was very unsettling knowing Rick's parents were stuck locally until their car was safe to drive, two days later. I had managed to avoid them. Their car was finally ready, and they would be heading out early the next morning. They wanted to meet with the family one final time to say goodbye. *Damn it!* I thought I was going to miss them. *Fine.*

We met at a neighborhood ice cream shop. Rick was already there with two of our kids. I was running behind from car-pooling kids to a school event. I took my sweet time – I did not want to be there. I entered the restaurant, mustered up a smile and said hello. There were two booths, across from each other. Rick Sr, Rick and his brother were sitting in a booth along with kids having conversation, jokes and dessert. Edna, my sister in-law, sitting in the booth directly across. I settled in at the table and tried to join the conversation but I had a very hard time pretending, and I was visibly uncomfortable. I hated that I had to sit at the same table. I tried to hide my restlessness, but it was impossible. I felt like I was suffocating. Everyone finally finished their desserts, and it was time for goodbyes, hugs and till next time. *Until never* for me.

Rick Sr. came in to hug me. I immediately felt outrage and went into defense mode. There way in hell I was going to let that nasty, bigot hug me. A ferocity took over me with a rush of heat, outrage boiling over me. I had never experienced an impulsive aggression. I pushed my arm forward, to stop him from coming in toward me. I said "I don't want a hug from you." Oblivious, he acted as if he was still coming to hug me, I didn't realize my voice was loud. I said "NO. You DON'T get to hug me. Not after your RACIST comment in my house."

My father in-law's eyes widened in surprise, but after a beat, he responded with "Whatever." He gave me his back to walk away. Just like Rick.

The moment happened in an instant. I heard dead silence and everything immediately went into slow motion. I remember every little nuance. Rick's eyes dark, turning to me in disbelief. My oldest, eyes wide, mouth open but the sides curled, as if to laugh. Edna was baffled and embarrassed. My youngest, shoulders dropped, we had just celebrated a milestone birthday, I felt the anger. The tables behind us turned their heads in our direction. The cashier leaned his gaze in our direction. My brother and sister in-law across the room looked dumbfounded.

Everyone made their way out of the ice cream shop as quickly as they could. Rick got in the car with the kids, and sped off. I got in my car, and followed at a very angry speed, clenching the wheel. I couldn't stop myself. It was the biggest emotional outburst I had ever had. And I didn't care! I laughed and laughed. At that moment in time, the words shot out of my mouth, I felt every one of my colorful ancestors standing and surrounding me. I felt all the times my people, my family and my culture were made to feel voiceless, marginalized and made fun of; it felt that they were heard too. I felt their power and pride.

Everything I had experienced with my in-laws over the years was bottled up for years, along with Rick's nasty behavior, and the upcoming divorce announcement, I unleashed, exploded and erupted wrath everywhere! I had listened and tolerated their toxic bullshit for years. *Fuck Them!* We arrived at our house. The battle was not over. I felt like I had just stood up for myself. I was stating the truth. My daughter's boyfriend was black. Was she going to hide him? I had lost it. And now I was the one being the crazy, abusive person? I heard it from my kids, they were yelling angrily. I embarrassed them, I hurt them. And for that I apologized, I felt terrible.

Things were going so wrong. Rick tried to guilt trip me to regain control, "After everything they have done for us. My father will never apologize." He was aiming to intimidate me and regain control. Both his hands in his pockets, his back straight. He was infuriated and was doing his best to be cool as he was intentionally derailing the conversation, antagonizing and invalidating me. I was not going to be manipulated. Not again. There was no way in hell I would ever apologize! I didn't lie. I was proud of myself. My rage was still fiery – I felt like I could take him. The anger and adrenaline was so big in my body, I wanted to hit him so badly. My feet were anchored into the floor, so heavy I had to hold my ground. I was almost willing to have a physical fight with my husband. Almost. I didn't take the bait. My children were home, and I didn't want to go to jail. I have no memory of how the night ended.

Coming down from this confrontation I fell back into distress and misery. Everyone in the house hated me. I felt like I was facing the future alone. It was another breaking point in my life. Rock bottom. It was devastating. It was so much! So much coming at me at once. It created suffering emotions and a bigger need for change.

I retreated. My solitude became my sacred space. The significance of solitude was profound in my journey. Sometimes it was a beautiful space. It's where I could slow down enough to hear the silence. It whispers. It is a place and process of self discovery. Free from all influences, where you can understand your thoughts, feelings, desires and fears. Finding that inner voice that is always drowned out. Alone, I confronted and embraced my reality and accepted it. It didn't happen overnight. Healing is always a work in progress. I was creating a deeper spiritual connection just through being still. It was affirming. I was fully present. Free to meet myself, flaws and all. Looking for clarity as I prayed. The only way to get to know yourself and to get into alignment is to be one hundred percent honest about who you are, about your experiences and to love yourself anyway. Then, radical self acceptance. That is something I still work on everyday.

I was on a mission. I had to move forward, in spite of fears. I was getting out of this sick marriage. I picked myself up, I dusted myself off. Trembling, I pulled myself together. We had our scheduled counseling session with Carol. I was going to serve Rick with divorce papers in her presence. I felt like I needed a witness. I discussed it with her in my previous session. I didn't know how he was going to react. We had not recovered from the family ice cream incident. My parents were also very concerned. They planned to sit in their car across the street in case I needed protection.

I sat in my normal seat for our session. We revisited the incident. I remember distinctly saying, "I refuse to live like this anymore." As if he was calling my bluff, Rick said "Oh, are you going to get a divorce." He made it so easy. I told him I filed right before his parents arrived. I handed him the papers. Carol sat in silence as our conversation unfolded.

Rick froze in disbelief. He didn't think I would ever do it. I pulled out the papers from my purse, handed them to him. For a moment, he appeared to shrink in his seat. He grabbed the papers, asked for a pen to sign. *Isn't he going to read it first?* For a minute he seemed off, as if he didn't know what to do next. He picked up the papers and walked out the door. I immediately texted my parents. It was done. But now I was afraid to leave. I was afraid to go home. I finished the session with Carol, and met my parents in the parking lot. I sat in the back of the car. I needed to go home, my kids were already in for the evening. I didn't know where Rick was or how long he would be gone. Or how he would be when he came home. I didn't think Rick had it in him to kill me, we did have guns in the house. I couldn't stop myself from going to that place. My parents decided to stay close and found a coffee shop. I don't remember driving home, but I made it there. My kids were safe and I was safe. Still, I grabbed a knife from the kitchen, took it to my bedroom. I locked the door behind me. I was not leaving my house.

Chapter Sixteen

After serving Rick with the divorce papers, the next few weeks became pugnacious. When we did speak – it was combative. We maintained our conversations private. The next big step was to tell our teenagers. We needed to do it, sooner than later. Even though they knew we were sleeping in separate rooms for months, hearing that your parents are ending their marriage is scary. Kids react to divorce in different ways. I spoke in detail to Carol about the best way to break the news. I researched and read as much as I could. I wanted to tell them gently, with kindness. I wanted to respect their emotions. I wanted to be supportive. Rick and I agreed to call a family meeting. We both made sure to tell them how loved they were. When we broke the news Rick and I were civil and calm.

Rick secured a lawyer. Found one, just as smug as him. We began to navigate through the complicated divorce process. The next few months Rick made my life so intentionally hellish. It was almost too much to handle. There was so much to do – maintain my emotions, educate myself on the divorce proceedings so I could manage myself in the process. The endless going back and forth gathering information, custody, property, assets, debt, support, bank state-ments, pay statements, taxes, phone calls, emails, schedules. I felt like I was being pushed to the edge meant to break me. Divorce is a huge life changing event.The worst part was feeling like I had no idea what I was doing – supposed to be doing. I often wondered how I was going to do this. I was teaching yoga classes, actively looking for a job, going to counseling, still trying to maintain a home. Most importantly, be a mom. The kids still needed dinner. I felt pulled in a million directions.

Things were moving forward, until Covid interrupted the divorce. The world came to a screaming halt. I was suddenly unem-ployed. With our already strained marriage, we quarantined. The arguments we had during the pandemic were some of our worst – hostile and contentious. We had opinions on Covid and how it could affect our children. Rick found driving around in the chaos of the pandemic as some sort of entertainment. Watching the stores empty and people begin to act a little crazy was like strange violence porn for him. *Who the hell he was becoming?*

Rick continued to avoid communication with me. It was as if he was intentionally digging his own grave. He had so many oppor-tunities to do right by me. He created this situation, living so much in his own ego, own imagination. I was no longer concerned with what he was doing, who he was engaging with. I no longer wanted that doubt.

I utilized my time during the pandemic by going through all our bills, statements, assets, cleaning house, decluttering. I stayed connected to family and friends. I continued to have my weekly visits with Carol. I'd stay up late into the night looking at deposits, withdrawals, and other strange activities. I was putting together some sort of puzzle, but I had no idea what it was.

Things seemed strangely quiet. On his day's off Rick would be gone all day. What was this new energy? He was extra sneaky. *Is he trying to be a player?* I realized it had been a year since we had remotely been intimate. My ability to sense what he was up to was always on point. I got the distinct feeling that he was with someone. I amped up my investigation, purchased a public records app for background checks and began doing people searches. It led me down the most interesting rabbit hole. One search led to the next, then the next. Dating profiles, phone numbers, connecting the dots. And there it was again. Right in front of my face! I tracked three women, but couldn't prove the fourth. Matched those strange banking transactions to locations close to the cities those women lived in. He left an easy trail to follow.

The realization of the discovery was different this time. I already knew who Rick was. He had shown me so many times that – I was detached from feeling. But why would he model this behavior to his kids? A father is a protector, a provider of stability and support, strong and valiant. Father's influence our relationship with ourselves and others. Children learn by watching, especially their parents.

My animosity for him grew immensely during the pandemic time. He declared me the villain of his own version of the story. I began to outgrow him even more. I was growing bolder and stronger and more tired of his shit. I was fired up. The times we argued, he would provoke a reaction out of me. I would lash back at him. It was destabilizing. Rick was malicious. His mission was to confuse me. He wanted me to give up. I was not him.

The silent treatment was the worst. Stonewalling is an often overlooked form of abuse. Rick intentionally ignored me, even in front of our kids. If we were in the kitchen together, he would intentionally keep his back to me. I frequently would imagine whacking him in the back of the head with a skillet. He was living at such a low level. He was trying his hardest to bring me down with him. Rick had the capacity to change, grow. He refused. He couldn't figure out how I was able to do the things I was able to do. His own underlying energy would often expose him. His eye contact, body language. The things that I said were scarily accurate and in sync with his emotional and mental process.

On one of the few occasions I needed to communicate with Rick, I asked if I could use his computer. I was applying for a job and needed to fill out some online forms. Rick hovered over my shoulder, till he realized that's what I was actually doing. Then he left me to do my task. I took care of what I needed to do, but took advantage of being on his computer. He left his email up.

Generally, text, phones, and emails are private. I know this. You shouldn't look without consent. I know this too. I didn't care. Immediately, I was appalled and disgusted. Rick had shared my very intimate private photos and a detailed conversation with a random internet troll named "Drunken Gentlemen." *What the hell am I looking at? He didn't delete the pictures. Liar.*

Thank God I was already sitting down, because I would have dropped to the ground. My husband, who I trusted to delete these personal photos, was sharing pictures of his wife with strangers. Strangers! I had my phone handy, I quickly took pictures of the emails and the pictures that he sent. I found another email, applying to be in a threesome with another couple. There were more. I immediately got off the computer. I was on the verge of another breakdown. .

I was afraid to look any further for fear of what else I might find. *Who in the hell was I married to? How was he even capable of this? What's wrong with him? What a piece of shit human I'm married to!* I was barely functioning. It was a severe blow. This was unthinkable to me. I wondered, *Did he delete any of the pictures from the past? Who else could he have shown? Where else could he have posted my personal pictures? What if that person shared my pictures?* I tried to search different sites, but my eyes burned from pornography. It was emotional warfare. He broke me again.

I shared with Carol at my next appointment. I then shared it with my lawyer. I could press charges against him, but it was out of her arena. I was a police matter now. I tried not to be scared, to refocus on getting out of the marriage as fast I could.

When the shock subsided, my anger and rage began to reappear. I despised him. *You are a father!!! How could he? What did he gain from behaving like this? What was he capable of with our kids?* He was already alienating me. It scared me that I wanted to kill him.

It took me a few days, maybe weeks to process everything. The person that I loved so deeply betrayed me again. I didn't deserve this. I was consumed with vehement rage. It took me about another week or so to build up the courage to contact the police. I left my house, pulled into a parking lot and paused to regroup. I had to breathe – I had to surround myself with divine protection.

This time, when I shared my story again, it was different. I told the police officer everything. Confidently. Without fear of judgment. I had no reason to be embarrassed. This was not my fault. Rick was out of control. The detective who listened kindly, gathered my information and told me it was nonconsensual pornography. It's completely illegal and known as distributing intimate images without consent. He just needed my statement, my address and they could pick him up and arrest him on charges of revenge porn. I was hanging on to a dangerously thin thread! I had to think smart. I couldn't do anything then. I felt like I was going to have a heart attack. I took the police officer's badge number and phone number, and said thank you hung up.

That was when I stopped judging myself for feeling stuck. I no longer questioned God about why I went through what I went through. I laid those burdens down. I was just now glad to experience another day. I began to feel a new sense of clarity. I was taking baby steps and growing stronger and moving forward. I was doing the work to create the path. Everyday I began to detach more and more. I had each foot in two different worlds. There was the expansion into the person I was trying to grow into but there was this constant pull back because of fear of the unknown.

Rick did a number on me. My psyche. My self esteem. My value. I was protecting myself. Love is supposed to be easy. Your ability to love is important. How you give it, and how you receive it. Being toxic is not attractive. Being a cheater is not attractive. Grow the fuck up.

On top of everything there was still a tremendous amount of stress with the pandemic and divorce, when I found out my ninety-nine year old Abuela contracted Covid. My mother contracted it from her. A few days later, I got the call that my father who lived out of the country was declining in health. Two of my parents were sick, and for the first time during the pandemic, I had family members with the virus. My anxiety flared. The reality of the pandemic hit home. The thought of losing both my parents scared the hell out of me. I reached out to my lawyer, I needed a couple of days. I had to slow down. I needed to regroup.

There was another delay to divorce. I was hit so hard. It would take me a year to recover and be able to finalize the divorce. Bad things really do come in threes.

I was about to get thrashed, and I didn't see it coming.

Chapter Seventeen

I suddenly and tragically lost my beloved younger brother. We had an amazing conversation the night before. Wine and chat was a regular event for us. Not just during the pandemic. I was always deeply connected to him. We confirmed our lunch the next day. I called on the way. Voice mail. And I called again. We had plans. Maybe his phone was dead. Maybe something came up. Mike would never stand me up. I parked next to his car when I arrived at his apartment. Something was not right. I knocked on the door. I banged on the door. I yelled at the door. I went back downstairs and stood below his second floor window and yelled. If I could have climbed the wall like Spider Man I would have. *This couldn't be happening. This wasn't supposed to happen!* The rest of the story, well, it's another story. Right now, I hold it in my heart.

Logically, we expect to lose our elderly family and friends first. He was one of the most important people in my life. He was my youngest sibling, my favorite person. We experienced our lives together. He was supposed to be there for the rest of my life. I was there the day he was born. I was there the day he left. It was the most traumatic loss of my life. It left me disoriented.

The grief was the most gut wrenching, painful emotion I had ever felt. My entire family – jolted into a new shattered existence. We didn't know who we were without him. I had the responsibility and honor of planning and executing his Celebration of Life. I went into a robotic survival mode. I never imagined that something could be harder than my current divorce circumstances.

One month later, I lost my Abuela. She was ninety-nine. She and I shared the same birthday. While it was somewhat expected, it was still a tragic loss in the middle of a tragic loss. On top of divorce. I had never seen a dead body, in real life. I had seen two in one month. You are never prepared for the death of your family. My world was unrecognizable.

One month later, I lost my father. He passed away alone. I did not get to say goodbye. I was unable to travel in the state that I was in. I watched his funeral online. My entire world as I knew it no longer existed. I was lost and directionless. Again, I was knocked down hard to my knees, landing in the biggest, ugliest grief I had ever experienced in my life. I fell into a deep sorrow.

The energy of death was dense. My season of grief led me to my biggest transformations. Through the process of grieving I became someone new. I lost so many people that were so important to me. I was uncomfortably, comfortable in the state of grief that was my everyday life. It was debilitating. There were so many days I could not get out of bed. Everything hurt, my entire body ached with anguish. Feeling the emotions came in intense, unpredictable waves. I felt so alone in my questions, gloom and mourning. Then, I would feel regret and numbness would drown me. I cried burning tears, scream cried, silent cried, angry cried, floods. My heart literally ached, from being cracked open. My chest hurt, I could barely breathe. My mind would race, then my heart would follow again. It was harrowing.

It made me realize that the time that was forced into rest, to heal from my health crisis, that I was being divinely placed in that period of isolation. I was building spiritual stamina and endurance. As if everything up until that point was a period of preparation. I still don't know how I survived the months after three major losses, back to back. I had three new guardian angels. My heart still aches.

True to his character, Rick ignored me. When I called him to tell him my brother had died, I could hear the confusion and shock in his silence. Rick was already void of any emotional capacity. He asked me if he should come over to the apartment where my brother lived. A real man would have said I'm on my way. I said "No." He had already let me down so many times. Later that night, after I broke the news to my kids, Rick walked past me and said "Sorry, for your loss." I was visibly distraught, swollen bloodshot eyes, red puffy face, sobbing and crying my eyes out. Rick met my brother when was two years old. He never offered my parents his condolences. I didn't want any comfort from him. But he didn't even try. Rick had been in my life since I was nineteen years old. *Was he really that heartless?*

Theresa and Ruby were the ones who came to be by my side. Always with food, wine, tissues and hugs. They held my hand, wiped my tears and loved and cared for me. I would not have survived if it were not for the caring and generosity of these two women. They held me up, when I had no strength to hold myself up. Theresa and Ruby are a huge part of my survival.

Parenting was extra complicated. When you are a parent, you are expected to show up, no matter what. That's what parents do. This was different. We had experienced the painful loss of family pets. My kids were experiencing their first major loss. There was no shielding them. My world was crumbling. I was already depleted. I regret that I could not be a stronger example and support for them during that time in our lives. I was so messy.

I had to rely on Rick again, to maintain the basics of running the household for our already broken family.

The months ahead were excruciating. I was raw. I struggled to function, even the basics. I couldn't remember if I brushed my teeth. I would over eat – or not eat at all. Even though I was in bed for long periods of time, I didn't sleep. The constant ache of grief severely fatigued me. I barely had energy to make it through a full day. I would have several breakdowns at any given moment. I saved my energy for when I was working, teaching my yoga classes that I loved so much. My divorce looming, I wanted to push through it. It felt like a constant hangover. The massive hole in my heart was so big. Rick and I continued to live separately in the same home for one year. Avoiding each other at all costs.

My counseling sessions with Carol began to go in a different direction. I was constantly tired. Not like being tired from a regular day, or a really bad day. It was a never ending emotional exhaustion. I lost myself even more. *Who am I now? What is this life? What should I do next?* I did not know how to go on. I had to allow my relationship with myself to evolve yet again.

This was not an easy process. Again, I was trying to relearn myself. I immersed myself deeper into my meditation and spiritual practice. I dedicated myself daily to healing, while grieving. It sustained me. Slowly, over time – all the things I was practicing, researching, had a way of leading me home to my soul, through my physical body. I was learning and living from my experience, and trusting. But not able to let go of what happened, all the while planning my next steps.

That time in my life was so strange. As though I was living a nightmare I could not wake up from. Deep down, I knew I was on the right track. It was a lot to carry but I was doing the best that I could at the time. I needed to do something with purpose, to come back to life, while preparing for my future. I invested and enrolled in additional yoga training. It provided more structure, knowledge and benefited my healing journey and career. It was a big challenge – physical and mental. But a huge accomplishment for me during the most difficult time of my life. It was a commitment of three hundred hours – I was immensely proud. Theresa and Ruby were the ones that celebrated with me.

My life was far from perfect, but I was resilient and was figuring out who I was going to be in the world. With my heart pounding, my hands shaking, it was time to finish what I started. We put our dream home on the market.

There were still more obstacles, serious challenges, more delays. There was so much damage. My life felt like a soap opera. Rick didn't stop his ways. He was insidious. He moved out before I did, taking only what he wanted and needed. He intentionally left, and did not come back. Our kids were in their late teens and decided where they wanted to live. It was heartbreaking when one of my kids left with him. And the dogs! My sweet dogs. I was mourning again. The dream house, the dream family, the dream life, all over.

I ended up selling, hauling, donating, gifting, giving away, trashing twenty years.

Everything had a memory attached to it. I certainly didn't want it. Rick left me with the added headache of cleaning out the house. Again, Theresa and Ruby came to my rescue. The adjustment period was difficult. Our beautiful house sold quickly. We completed a difficult mediation to finalize our divorce. The final push on an arduous journey. Every fiber of my being felt stretched to its limits. The process was grueling. I felt as if I was hit by a train.

It was finally happening. I was on the edge of leaping forward. The last stretch was the most demanding. I was feeling a deep weariness, but I was closer than ever. I embraced the exhaustion, and took the final steps. There was a surge of excitement and fear that propelled me forward. I scrambled to find a new place to live, move, settle.

I met so many beautiful versions of myself along this journey and shed so many layers. It was a painful process of letting go. Including important people and relationships. I could have given up. It takes a deep level of surrender and trust to move forward. My new life required me to step into new territory. Everything was unfamiliar. The way I felt about myself, the way I viewed life. It was time to expand again. I was leading my life on faith and excited for my future of endless possibilities.

I celebrate and cherish my journey. It was a profound alignment to reclaim myself.

Chapter Eighteen

I used to think my story was rare and unique. Now I know someone else needs to hear my experience. The purpose of sharing my story is to help others who may be living similar circumstances. To unchain myself. To let others know, they are not alone. To provide hope and encouragement to those that remain silent.

The calling of my life has been different. My soul was requiring a new life. I was seeing myself for the first time. Seeing myself properly – honoring myself with all my beautiful scars. I didn't have to hide anymore. I refused. I own all those parts of me as sacred. I know now that it was part of my growth and evolution as a woman. I was tested on every level possible.

It took a long time for me to come to a place of harmony in my new life. There was so much to recover from. I released opinions other people had about the way my life may have looked. I had to re-establish my sense of safety and trust – first with myself, then with others. When the shock would subside, intense emotions and fears would resurface. Once we were officially divorced, there was still lingering sadness, depression, exhaustion, stress, anxiety and PTSD.

The recovery process from trauma is ongoing. It affected my nervous system, my thought process, my ability to make decisions. Healing from trauma and abuse is constant and complex. It requires effort, patience, grace, therapy, family, friends and so much unconditional love. Slowly and over time, I was able to rebalance myself, little by little, each day different. Finding peace was not easy. There was pain getting to that peace. Peace costs a lot. I am forever sorry to my children for all the hurt that came out of this. It wasn't supposed to be this way. I had to protect myself. I am sorry.

I was transformed from the inside out. I found the strength and fortitude to be misunderstood by others, especially those closest to me. It takes courage to be judged and ridiculed. I shed so many layers, over and over again. I built myself from the ground up. More than once.

The doubts and fears still reappear from time to time. I just don't believe them anymore. I can hold my head proudly, healed and still healing, knowing I am stronger than I was, wiser than I was. It's a beautiful thing to recognize and appreciate myself. To be comfortable in my skin. I am human. I've made mistakes. I ask for forgiveness. I love hard and I fight hard. I learned to clearly understand myself in order to understand what I was deserving of. I'm still learning to master my confidence, my voice and live my life in peace.

I wish you the same in your journey and so much love.

Conclusion

You cannot use normal rules for abnormal relationships. Rick and I had a narrow view when we began exploring. We had no idea what we were doing. We did not consider family, work, parenting, personal feelings, friendships, reactions. Our discussions were all imaginary scenarios.

We did not define any rules when it came to HotWifing. If you are experiencing a similar circumstance, it is important to do more than just absorb my story. Do you recognize yourself? Do you identify with some of the same feelings? It is important to pause, and sort through feelings, impressions, and assumptions.

How do you function in the real world, maintain the rest of your life and responsibilities, if you can't communicate and function on a basic level with your spouse? It has a ripple effect. It eventually will trickle into everything in your life.

If you decide to explore this lifestyle, I hope you dedicate time and energy to plan. If you don't plan, don't be surprised if you lose everything. Ultimately, the decision to become a HotWife is yours, and yours alone. It is not consent if you keep saying no, and he keeps asking till you give in.

I applied many tools to heal, grow and change. Therapy and medication with a professional, yoga and meditation, somatic breathing, journaling, rest, grace, true friendships, prayer, nature. There are so many ways to heal. There is no right or wrong way. There is not a magic pill or one-size-fits – all quick fix. Everyone's journey is their own. There is no timeline to healing. It is a constant choice every day. It requires intention, effort, and dedication.

Yoga began for me as a physical routine. It was amazing how it made me feel better and healthier overall. I was going every day, and I loved that I felt better about myself. I loved it so much I had to keep learning.

I was surprised how powerful meditation was when I first began to explore it. The stillness and controlled breathing. The sensation of energy felt tingling and warm. Paying attention to my breath helped the meddling thoughts settle. Each experience was different. I experienced profound feelings of peace. Being aware and in the moment was what allowed me to become more observant in my day-to-day life.

Somatic breathing was and is still a huge part of my healing practice. You can go without food or water for a few days. You can't go very long without breathing. I learned this technique through different yoga training, personal research and practices and made it my own. For me it promoted a deeper awareness in the present moment. It can guide you into deeper relaxation that guides your body release tension and ease stress.

Journaling for me was a way of planning, organizing, and being productive. But then, it evolved into gathering thoughts, expressing emotions. It helped me gain perspective, as if I was giving myself advice and answering my own questions.

If you personally are trying to implement healing in your journey, be honest with yourself. The story you believe about yourself and your relationship are a big part of healing.

Decide what it means to you. Break down doubts, judgements, expectations, interpretations, and assumptions to better understand yourself. What should you consider? What boundaries will you put into place?

Reflecting on your experiences, your values, your daily interactions can bring you more clarity. Everything really is that deep. Take inventory of your marriage. How can you get to the heart of the circumstances you are dealing with? Acknowledge and accept where you are. What can you shift around to make yourself feel better?

This can be a difficult and awkward process to explore. If it brings up painful emotions and makes you feel worse, there is no need to push yourself. Take small steps. Take what you need; leave what you don't.

Only you have the power to speak over your life.

Define your rules. Commit to them. Believe what you see.

Afterword

There are times we say or do things we wish he had not. Mistakes happen. Life happens. If we don't share our experiences, how will we grow and support one another? Be gentle and kind to yourself. Give yourself so much love. Writing this book was something I never dreamed of doing, but my heart would not stop nudging me forward. It was born in a space of gratitude, love and acceptance. Through writing my story, I was able to honor, understand and innerstand myself with grace, strength and determination to evolve and expand. It was a difficult and beautiful process of letting go. True empowerment comes from walking your walk, and talking your talk. Remember who you are.